Without Fear of Being Happy

Without Fear of Being Happy

Lula, the Workers Party and Brazil

EMIR SADER
and
KEN SILVERSTEIN

VERSO

London · New York

Verso
UK: 6 Meard Street, London W1V 3HR
USA: 29 West 35th Street, New York, NY 10001-2291

Verso is the imprint of New Left Books

British Library Cataloguing in Publication Data

Sader, Emir, *1943–*
  Without fear of being happy : Lula, the
  Workers Party and Brazil.
  I. Title II. Silverstein, Ken
  324.281074

  ISBN 0-86091-306-6
  ISBN 0-86091-523-9 pbk

Library of Congress Cataloging-in-Publication Data

Sader, Emir,
    Without fear of being happy : Lula, the Workers Party and Brazil
  Emir Sader and Ken Silverstein,
      p.   cm.
    Includes index.
    ISBN 0-86091-306-6. — ISBN 0-86091-523-9 (pbk.)
    1. Partido dos Trabalhadores (Brazil)—History. 2. Lula, 1945–
      3. Brazil—Politics and government—1964-1985. 4. Brazil—
  Politics and government—1985– I. Silverstein, Ken, II. Title.
  JL2498.T7S23   1991
  324.281'07'09—dc20
  91-25893

Typeset by York House Typographic Ltd, London.
Printed in Great Britain at Biddles Ltd, Guildford.

Contents

Acknowledgements

To Bel and Luciana.
   E.S.

To the *posseiros* of the Parrot's Beak and, for general help, encouragement and support, to Clara Rivera, JoAnn Wypijewski and Alexander Cockburn.
   K.S.

Both authors would like to thank Clara Rivera and Sueann Caulfield, who translated Emir Sader's section of the book from the Portuguese.

Introduction

With a worldwide turn to neo-liberalism taking place, this may seem a strange time to be writing a book about a radical socialist party. The countries of Eastern Europe are not only abandoning Stalinism, but are throwing themselves head-first into the full restoration of capitalism. In Poland, Solidarity leader Lech Wałęsa red-baits striking workers. Czechoslovak President Václav Havel advocates total adherence to US foreign policy goals, and Hungary's economic path appears to be that proposed by the likes of Milton Friedman and George Gilder. This embrace of capitalism is not terribly hard to understand. The communist governments of Eastern Europe did not construct political or economic models that met the needs of their populations, nor did they enjoy a broad base of popular support.

More surprisingly, though, the left is also largely in retreat in Latin America, as many countries in the region emerge from decades of dictatorial right-wing military rule. Argentine Peronist Carlos Saúl Menem is looking more and more like the Margaret Thatcher of the Pampas; in Peru, the left did not even manage to win a place in the June 1990 presidential runoff election; and Venezuelan "Social Democrat" Carlos Andres Pérez was so ardent in implementing International Monetary Fund-style policies in 1988 that bloody riots resulted. Even in Chile, where the Pinochet regime was finally brought down after sixteen years of rule, President Patricio Alywin has promised to maintain free-market economic policies. And leftists received only 23 per cent of the December 1989 congressional vote, as against 40 per cent in the last election before Salvador Allende was overthrown in 1973.

1

This trend may not be ideological or permanent. Latin economies are in such chaos – partly because of a regional foreign debt of $450 billion – that only one of South America's civilian presidents of the past decade (Virgílio Barco of Colombia) has been able to elect his own successor. Furthermore, part of the left's difficulties are, without doubt, attributable to the murder of thousands of opposition political leaders by the dictatorships which ruled in much of the region for the past three decades, as well as the brutal repression of socialist organizing. But whatever the reasons, in most Latin American countries the left finds itself in an unfavourable position, both electorally and otherwise.

In Brazil, though, which at first glance appears to follow the pattern, the left is not only alive and well, but growing. The presidential election of December 17, 1989 – the first direct vote for president in twenty-nine years – brought conservative populist Fernando Collor de Mello to power. Collor, who was inaugurated in March 1990 replaced immensely unpopular right-wing president José Sarney, who took office following an Electoral College vote strongly influenced by the 1964 to 1985 military regime.

But what was most significant about the vote was Collor's narrow five-point margin of victory over Luís Inácio Lula da Silva of the Partido dos Trabalhadores (PT or Workers Party). Da Silva's campaign represented the first time that a radical party inextricably linked to the working class and popular organizations – and led by a worker – had ever threatened to take power by electoral means. The PT's platform for the campaign – which called for the break-up of the huge unproductive estates that dominate the countryside, in order to benefit Brazil's estimated 12 million landless peasants; a "democratization," but not privatization, of the large and often corrupt state sector; and an end to the country's export-led model of economic growth, with an emphasis on meeting domestic needs – was indeed a revolutionary call for change.

In a pre-election issue, the major news weekly *Veja* noted nervously that neither a party like the PT nor a candidate like Lula had ever before had a realistic chance of taking power in the country. "Collor could be elected and conduct a great or disastrous administration, but no one is nervous about his program – in either case, there is a certainty that Brazilian society, in its fundamental points, will be more or less the same as it was before. The hypothesis of Lula . . . is different. Like Collor, he could be elected and has, at least in theory, the same mathematical chances of running a good or bad government. But there is no doubt that it will be a government completely different than all previous ones," the magazine speculated.[1]

The 1989 election was no isolated phenomenon. The PT's birth in the late 1970s, and its growth into the country's most solidly established political party, is tied to the transformations Brazil underwent during the period of military rule. While the country's economy expanded rapidly, and a high degree of industrialization took place, social inequalities – among the worst in the world – worsened dramatically. The PT grew out of these developments, and brings together radical unionists, landless peasants, shantytown activists and the progressive wing of the country's powerful Roman Catholic Church. While the party was initially based in São Paulo, the country's industrial and financial center – where both labor and capital are strongest – it expanded throughout the country during the conservative-led transition to civilian rule that culminated with the December 1989 election.

The PT is without question the largest explicitly socialist political party in South America, and its growth, particularly in the almost pre-capitalist countryside, is unprecedented in the region. With Lula's strong showing (he received 31 million votes for president), and with the PT already in control of three of the country's largest cities, the party is helping lead the opposition to the Collor government and is poised to launch a strong bid for power in the years ahead.

But the PT is far more than an average political party, and in many ways more closely resembles a social movement. The party and its activists are deeply involved with organizations fighting for social change throughout the country, particularly those promoting workers' rights, agrarian reform and better living conditions in the slums (or *favelas*) that ring the large cities. In many rural areas, there is literally no line between these social movements and the party itself. Also, the PT brings together various, and often quarrelling, factions, that somehow manage to resolve their disputes democratically, and without tearing the party apart. As one observer wrote:

What is at stake here is a new type of party whose significance and interest extend beyond Brazil. It is not a matter of a social democratic party directed by parliamentarians, organized as an electoral machine with the usual neo-Keynesian reformist program and Atlanticist orientation. Nor is this a bureaucratic communist party with its omnipotent apparatus, its political and ideological submission to the USSR; it is not a populist party, such as Peronism or the old Partido Trabalhista Brasileiro (PTB – Brazilian Labor Party), directed by charismatic bourgeois politicians with a vaguely nationalist program and corrupt bureaucracy of "yellow" labor union political bosses. Finally, it is not a self-styled revolutionary sect, organized on the margins of the real workers' movements and bound up in dogma and rigid rituals. In reality, it is difficult to find analogues and equivalents.[2]

Whatever the difficulty in labeling the party, the PT's coalition of forces represents a Brazilian "New Left," and is certainly the most hopeful model for democratic socialism anywhere in South America.[3]

In addition to describing the PT's birth, development, and ideological positions, this book will attempt to show how the broader Brazilian context offers great possibilities for the growth of a party such as the PT and at the same time presents difficult obstacles. The Brazilian elite – unlike their counterparts elsewhere in South America – have never faced a genuine revolutionary threat. Independence was declared by a renegade member of the Portuguese court, and the monarchy was overthrown in a bloodless coup led by the military. "Civil society" has traditionally been very weak, the military has long exercised tremendous power – directly and indirectly – and the economic elite have rarely faced organized worker opposition. (Of critical importance in recent years, the nation's media is thoroughly dominated by the elite. Especially noteworthy is the TV Globo network, privately owned but in practice little more than a slick, sophisticated and highly effective Ministry of Propaganda.)

At the same time, Brazil's notorious poverty offers fertile ground for the PT's growth. And since the country's ruling class must surely rate as one of the greediest and most corrupt of the twentieth century, radical political changes such as those proposed by the party have a wide appeal with the poor. The PT's skillful navigation through this terrain is central to its strength, and has helped lead to a growing mobilization and organization of the popular sectors – in unions, Christian Base Communities, neighborhood associations, and so on. In short, "civil society," while still weak in comparison with advanced capitalist nations (and even a majority of Latin American countries), has begun to emerge.

Also of key importance to the party's story is the crucial role played by da Silva – a northeastern migrant to São Paulo, former metal-worker and union leader, who led huge strikes against foreign-owned automobile manufacturers in the late 1970s, and is certainly the most important labor leader in Brazil's history.

Finally, as is the case in much of Latin America, the role of Catholic Church leaders and activists is absolutely crucial to understanding Brazilian politics, and the development of the PT. The Church's role is especially important in Brazil, as its hierarchy – unlike anywhere else in the world and despite being increasingly divided – is largely supportive of the so-called "preferential option for the poor," and the country is the cradle of Latin American liberation theology (Brazil's progressive church leaders are far more powerful than their counterparts in Nicaragua ever were).

With the left in many places in the world in crisis, an analysis of the PT's experience and problems is especially important. Although it should be unnecessary to point this out, the current gloating among conservatives makes it imperative to note that, at least for the Third World, capitalism has hardly produced spectacular results, other than widespread poverty. Inter-American Development Bank statistics show that nine of twelve South American countries registered a decline in per capita GNP during the 1980s.[4] Behind those statistics are such horror stories as the development, due to chronic malnutrition, of a race of pygmies in Brazil's northeast, one of the poorest regions in the Western hemisphere. In neighboring Peru, at least in the late 1970s, many of the poor were so desperate they had to survive on Nicovita, a substance used to fatten chickens. In Chile a 1986 study by the Academy of Christian Humanism showed that 86 per cent of the residents of two poor Santiago neighborhoods did not eat enough to sustain life. And in Argentina, one million children in Buenos Aires province alone go hungry.

What the PT's growth shows is that the current conventional wisdom in the First World is absurd, particularly when seen from the South. The "end of history" is not at hand; capitalism has not triumphed over socialism; and the International Monetary Fund's recipe for unequal economic growth is not the only path to development open to the Third World.

Three final points should be made. First, the "Lula" in da Silva's name was originally a nickname, which he had incorporated into his full legal name for electoral purposes (it could not appear on the ballot otherwise). "Lula" is how he is universally known and it is also how he will be referred to throughout this book.

Second, the book's title, "Without Fear of Being Happy," was the PT's slogan for the 1989 presidential campaign. According to Ricardo Kotscho, Lula's press aide, the slogan was part of a strategy to "overcome society's fear. The fear of the new. The fear of change."[5]

Third, in mid 1990, Lula, then serving out the last few months of his first term as a federal deputy from São Paulo state, announced he would not be a candidate in the October 1990 congressional elections. Saying he was frustrated by his experience in Congress, he has been travelling throughout the country, working with labor groups and popular organizations and, though not officially stated, preparing for a new shot at the presidency in 1994.

Lula's decision certainly resulted in electoral losses for the PT in October 1990 voting (he received over 650,000 votes in 1986, more than any other federal deputy, and has extremely broad coat-tails). Though the party doubled its number of federal deputies to thirty-five and elected its first ever Senator, Eduardo Suplicy from São Paulo state, the overall results were disappointing in light of the party's near triumph in the previous year's presidential race.

But Lula was betting on the long term. Opposition to the neo-liberalism now reigning throughout the region is centered in the unions, professional groups, neighborhood associations, Christian Base Communities, and other organized sectors – exactly those which form the PT's heart and whose strength must be increased if the challenge to new president Collor's policies is to be mounted.

Political commentators in Brazil predicted that poor electoral results would spell ruin for the party. But, as old newspaper archives perused while researching this book revealed, predictions of the PT's demise have been made in droves ever since the party was launched ten years ago. Since then, the PT has grown, slowly but surely, into one of the country's leading political forces. Based on the past record of the "experts," the PT has a long life ahead.

NOTES

1. *Veja*, November 29, 1989

2. Michael Löwy, "The Brazilian PT," *Latin American Perspectives*, Fall 1987, p.454.

3. The party is an inspiration to leftists throughout the region. In mid 1990, Luiz Zamora, an Argentinian socialist, said, "The PT is an extraordinary victory for Brazilian workers." At the time, the country's habitually divided left was discussing

the creation of a new party, to be named the "Partido de los Trabajadores." *Folha de São Paulo*, May 20, 1990.

4. Among the steepest drops were those registered by Argentina ($3,404.9 to $2,722.2); Mexico ($2,871.9 to $2,608.2); Venezuela ($5,224.8 to $4,617.2); and Peru (($1,716.5 to $1,241.0). In Brazil, the figure dropped from $2,480.5 to $2,471.4.

In Chile, per capita GNP climbed in the 1980s from $2,448.1 to $2,687.5. But that meager increase came after two brutal Pinochet-created recessions, and also at the expense of growing social inequality.

5. *Sem Medo de Ser Feliz*, Scritta Oficina Editorial, São Paulo 1990.

1

A Country with No Leftist Tradition

The growing strength of the Partido dos Trabalhadores on the Brazilian political scene does not represent the continuation of a long process of growth on the part of the Brazilian left. On the contrary, it stems from a "privilege of lateness." When the party began organizing in 1979, almost a decade had passed since the country's historically weak left had been wiped out by the military regime of 1964 to 1985. The Brazilian Communist Party, outlawed but operating clandestinely since 1947, had lost expression even earlier, soon after the coup itself.

In addition to the left's political weakness, the years before the PT's birth were marked by an expansive cycle of economic growth, which transformed the face of the country, accelerating industrialization, urban concentration and social inequalities. A new correlation of forces resulted, in which economic interests, especially labor, were markedly under-represented on the political front. Thus, the PT grew from a relatively "blank slate," and at such a point in time that it was possible to avoid ideological and practical errors made by past progressive movements, both in Brazil and elsewhere.

Compared with countries in the Southern Cone, the growth of both Brazilian unionism and leftist organizing is a relatively new phenomenon. The national economy was based on coffee production until 1929, and the principal form of labor employed was that of migrant rural workers, who were dispersed and easily controlled by landowners. Other countries with raw material export economies gave birth to an industrialized working class far earlier than did Brazil. In

9

Chile, for example, the production of minerals led to the emergence of an industrial proletariat early in the century. The process of urbanization and industrialization only got underway in Brazil with Getúlio Vargas's rise to power in 1930, and the first movement towards import substitution development.[1]

Prior to this, in the first decades of the century, a small proletarian movement tied to the non-durable consumer goods sector (especially shoes, clothing, alcohol and hats) had arisen. Prominent in organizing these workers were militant anarchist and socialist immigrants from Europe, notably Italy, Portugal and Spain. Just as elsewhere on the continent, the 1919 Bolshevik triumph in Russia accelerated the founding of a local Communist Party, which split the workers' movement. The sector tied to the new CP quickly became its most dynamic element.

However, popular mobilizations in the late 1920s, which were linked to protests against the oligarchic regime of Washington Luís, were not led, or even greatly influenced, by the budding workers' movements or the left. Junior officers of the armed forces, headed by Vargas, led the opposition to the Luís government, in a context of the growing political strength of urban populations and the middle class. In the 1930 presidential election, Luís's would-be successor, Julio Prestes de Albuquerque, defeated Vargas, obtaining about one million votes versus 700,000 for the latter. But Vargas's supporters cried fraud, deposed President Luís, and installed "Getúlio," as he is still popularly known.

The Communist Party itself, faced with real-life situations not addressed by the documents of the International and the ongoing process of Stalinization in the Soviet Union, was overtaken by events and saw its political profile gradually lowered. Only in the mid-1930s, when Luís Carlos Prestes, an important junior army officer, joined the CP, went to Moscow, and returned at the head of an insurrectional movement, did local communists attain any real prominence on the political scene.

The 1935 uprising Prestes led was, from a strategic standpoint, midway between the leftist line of the International's "Third Period" and its more recent one of the "Popular Front," elaborated in 1935 at the 7th Congress. The chosen method of struggle was insurrectional, with organized groups inside the barracks, supported externally by cells from the so-called National Liberation Alliance, tied to the CP and allied forces. The political line, on the other hand, was extracted from the International's call for an anti-fascist front, leaving aside such concepts as "class against class."

The Prestes-led uprising represents one of the few times in Brazilian history that the left addressed the question of power, even if in putschist form. However, the movement's plans were discovered by Vargas early on, leading to its early defeat and the arrest of Prestes and many other communist leaders.

The left, and mass movements, remained marginal to the political scene for the following ten years, until Vargas fell from power in 1945. The CP participated in that year's elections, and achieved a significant degree of support: its presidential candidate, Yedo Fiuza, received 10 per cent of the vote, finishing first in the key northeastern state of Pernambuco. Prestes was elected as a senator, along with fourteen federal deputies. In the Constituent Assembly, the CP won 8.6 per cent of the seats, just below the 10.2 per cent controlled by Vargas's Brazilian Labor Party (this was, however, far below the strength of the Social Democratic Party and the National Democratic Union, the two biggest parties, which held 40.9 per cent and 25.4 per cent of the seats, respectively).

In local elections held in 1947, the CP elected the largest bloc of deputies in Rio de Janeiro, then capital of the country, as well as in Santos, the major port. The party had eight daily newspapers, two publishing houses, and 180,000 militants. This important experience for the Brazilian left lasted only two years, from 1945 to 1947, when the Eurico Dutra government enlisted in the Cold War, broke ties with the Soviet Union and outlawed the CP again.[2]

From that point on, the CP (acting underground) developed an "anti-imperialist and anti-feudal" line, allying themselves with whatever faction of the bourgeoisie they considered "progressive," and pushed for nationalistic policies, including an agrarian reform which, according to official thinking, would open the path for socialism. On this basis, the CP supported the elected governments of Getúlio Vargas (1950-54). Juscelino Kubitschek (1955-60) and João Goulart (1961-64), emphasizing the organization of workers in state-controlled industries.

The rest of the left had little importance in political life, and neither did popular movements. Unions in the state sector were the movement's most dynamic element, but labor had little weight nationally (and practically none in rural areas where workers remained dispersed and unorganized). The possibility for independent action by unions was extremely limited, as the country's labor code and paternalistic structure, designed by Vargas when he first took power in 1930, and which remained largely intact, was based on Mussolini's Fascist model.

The most important social and political transformations prior to the PT's rise to national prominence took place in the 1960s. During João Goulart's government, the strength of the labor movement slowly grew, even reaching into the interior. Within the left, movements more radical than the CP were developing. The first Maoist split in the world took place in Brazil, resulting from a Stalinist division within the CP. Also born was a radical Catholic movement that later would ally itself with the Maoists, and a socialist Leninist group. These movements, though, remained marginal while the CP's official line was formally wedded to Goulart's government.

Of course, the most dramatic changes took place following the 1964 military takeover – which signified the failure of the Communist Party's practice of making alliances with "progressive" sectors of the ruling class: the Brazilian bourgeoisie, with few exceptions, solidly backed the armed forces.

The coup sparked a vigorous debate among progressives, focusing on the CP, which until then had played such a central role in the history of the Brazilian left. The debate centered on the most promising way to achieve revolutionary transformations in the country, at a time when national capitalism had chosen dictatorship, not democracy, as a means of promoting development. The climate in Brazil was permeated by international influences, especially those coming from Latin America. While on the continent capitalism showed itself incapable of redressing popular demands, Cuba offered a socialist alternative, presenting proposals for such crucial questions as health care, education and culture, as well as affirming its national sovereignty in the face of American imperialism.

Latin American guerrilla movements, already gaining strength in Venezuela, Peru, Colombia and Guatemala, appeared to be viable means of achieving anti-capitalist revolutions in every country on the continent. The figure of Che Guevara would later come to personify this image, made brighter by the action of Fidel's Cuba as a continent-wide catalyst of anti-imperialist struggle.

In a more general sense, the Vietnamese resistance to US imperial aims initiated the alignment of political and cultural figures in a broad grouping of the best humanity had to offer. To support Vietnam, Cuba, China, Latin American revolutionary movements and Che

Guevara, was to be on the side of revolution, of history, of justice and ethics.

The Brazilian debate was skewed by the pressure of events in Latin America. The appeal of an immediate call to armed struggle became stronger and stronger, as a result of a number of factors. First, there was the closing by the military regime of virtually all channels of legal institutional opposition, along with the generals' obvious intent to remain in power indefinitely (in contrast to their initial promises of a brief tenure) and construct an exclusionary regime.

Second, the maturing of guerrilla movements in other countries in the region occurred, especially in Uruguay (the Tupamaros) and Argentina, in addition to those previously mentioned. Solidarity with countries and movements in struggle in the Third World, coordinated by groups such as Tricontinental and the Cuban-based Latin American Organization of Solidarity, amplified the echo of revolutionary movements and strengthened the appeal for others to follow in their footsteps.

Third, the fragile nature of the Brazilian left's political experience, and the resulting lack of practical knowledge, permitted the debate rapidly to head towards "solutions" that favored armed struggle, in place of building a still incipient popular movement to counter the military's rule.

Within the CP, still the most important left organization, prominent radical leader Carlos Marighella went to Cuba to attend a meeting for continental solidarity and returned proposing that discussion be ended and armed struggle begun. His position was supported by a majority of party militants, especially those from youth groups. Opposition to such a stance did emerge, especially among the CP's long-time militants, but had the backing of only a minority. The same rush to armed struggle took place in other leftist groups; those who favored strengthening social movements were marginalized and heavily criticized.

Meanwhile, popular opposition to the regime was scattered and unorganized. Unions, which previously had been closely linked to the state via the Labor Ministry, quickly lost their voice as state support (albeit of a paternalistic nature) turned to persecution. Student groups were the first to retake to the streets after the coup, and they supplied the lion's share of militants to leftist groups. However, their contact with urban and rural workers was minimal. A small amount of clandestine organizing took place during the regime's early years in power, which led to several important strikes being called in 1968. But the stoppages were isolated, and received little support from other sectors.

Within this context, the more important groups proposing immediate armed struggle – the National Liberation Alliance, led by Marighella, and the Popular Revolutionary Vanguard, headed by ex-army captain Carlos Lamarca – launched "armed propaganda" actions. The execution of soldiers, bank robberies and assaults, were initiated to prepare the ground for the development of urban and rural guerrilla movements.

After a few spectacular actions, the most famous being the 1969 kidnapping of US ambassador Charles Elbrick and his exchange for fifteen political prisoners, the regime prepared a counterattack, which was facilitated by the guerrillas' lack of ties to the fragile popular movements. The government closed down Congress, decreed tougher and more repressive measures and went on the military offensive. Marighella and several other guerrilla leaders were killed in ambushes soon after.

By the end of 1969, the armed opposition was already virtually eliminated. With no real roots in social movements, disorganized and focusing on direct clashes with security forces – precisely the strong point of the dictatorship – the guerrillas launched a series of attacks from which they emerged badly beaten. The CP's Maoists would still attempt to forge a rural guerrilla movement, headquartered in the southeastern Amazon and based on the concept of encircling the cities from the interior, but their difficulties were even greater because the government had thoroughly consolidated its control in the interior.

By 1973, the military reigned supreme. The radical left had been completely crushed, its principal organizations eliminated and the majority of its fighters put out of combat – dead, imprisoned or exiled. Guerrilla groups were wiped out as political organizations. The faction of the CP which had opposed armed struggle was equally victimized by the repression, and lost the small amount of influence it had possessed before the coup.

Outside the country, too, a sense of defeat was brewing. Brazilian militants, initially centered in Chile, were dispersed after the 1973 coup that overthrew Salvador Allende, with the majority resettling in Western Europe.

In Latin America, the first cycle of guerrilla warfare was ending, mostly in defeat, further heightening the sense that the revolutionary tide was ebbing.

In Brazil, internal opposition to the generals was shifting from the radical left to the realm of Congress. Until the mid 1970s the pretence at democracy mounted by the regime (which included regularly scheduled elections for most elected positions) had led to electoral protests – abstentions, casting blank votes, and so on. The year after the coup, the government had decreed a law which banned all former parties and created just two new ones, the pro-government National Renovation Alliance (ARENA) and the official opposition, the Brazilian Democratic Movement (MDB). The latter brought together a wide ideological coalition of the regime's opponents, without attracting much popular interest or support. Protest votes almost always outnumbered votes for the MDB.

After the definitive defeat of the guerrilla movements, though, the MDB began to be an important focus for the opposition. The party's electoral force slowly grew, until in 1974 (precisely the moment at which then president General Ernesto Geisel assumed power and announced a "slow, but certain" political liberalization) it was able, for the first time, to win more congressional votes than ARENA. Although Congress had been stripped of most of its rightful powers, the MDB's increased representation signified the first institutional disapproval of the regime, accentuating internal problems for the government and strengthening those voices denouncing its economic policies and political repression.

The second half of the 1970s was marked by the strengthening of the institutional opposition, and by the slow reorganization of student and worker movements, as well as human rights organizations. Thus, the vacuum left by the virtual disappearance of the previously existing left began to be filled.

The thorough rupture with Brazil's "old left" is crucial to understanding the PT's birth and future trajectory. In addition to its political and generational distance from previous leftist organizations, there was also a general distrust of and disagreement with those elements of the left that survived the early years of repression and reemerged as the political opening widened. Both wings of the reborn Communist Party were thoroughly different from the PT, in terms of doctrine and political practice; also, the PT consciously avoided too rigid a definition in terms of socialist ideology.[3]

While ideological continuities certainly existed between the PT and the "old left," the most obvious being that both were anti-capitalist, the most outstanding element in the party's founding and growth is a break with left tradition. In fact, PT leaders did not initially consider the party to represent a new chapter in the Brazilian left's history.

NOTES

1. The end of the old regime resulted from an economic crisis tied directly to the collapse of the price of coffee on the international market, which itself resulted from the depression that rocked the United States and Europe after 1929. Coffee prices fell from 22.5 to 8 cents per pound during the next two years and Brazil's foreign exchange earnings were reduced by two-thirds between 1929 and 1932. Even with the drop in price, sales plunged. In 1930, 26 million bags of coffee were in storage, double the amount of Brazil's normal export volume. The foreign exchange crisis that resulted forced the country to use up all of its gold reserves to finance imports. E. Bradford Burns, *A History of Brazil*, Columbia University Press, p. 395.

2. Claudio Gurgel, *Estrelas e borboletas*, Editora Papagaio, p. 33.

3. The great majority of surviving guerrilla fighters joined the PT, having abandoned their strategy of armed struggle. Even several small sectarian groups, generally Trotskyite but some Maoist, adhered to the PT, seeing it as an important leftist front and a place to organize.

But that integration did not signify a marked continuity with the past. First, the number of such militants was extremely small, and the PT was dominated by its labor wing. Also, the party explicitly renounced armed struggle, and, from the very start, preached an anti-capitalism based on a workers' vanguard.

2

Economic Transformation and
Political Opposition

Entering the 1990s, the PT is certainly the most important independent leftist political party anywhere in the region. Its rapid growth is
particularly remarkable in a country like Brazil, whose history is one
of continuities rather than ruptures, where pacts among the elites, not
open conflicts, are the norm. Brazil's political independence, contrary
to what occurred in most of Latin America, was not achieved by war
against Iberian invaders, but was simply declared by a renegade
member of the Portuguese court in 1822. As legend and standard
history texts have it, Dom Pedro I, son of Portuguese Emperor Dom
João VI, who was given charge of Brazil, was riding horseback
between the cities of Santos and São Paulo with a small retinue when
he was overtaken by a messenger bearing letters from Portugal. One
informed him that the Cortes (the Portuguese parliament) had reduced
his powers. On the bank of the Ipiranga river, Dom Pedro, dressed in
steel-blue military garb, reared up on his majestic horse, puffed out
his chest and cried, "Independence or death!" Though modern-day
historians dispute some of the details – claiming that based on the
terrain and the heat, Dom Pedro was likely to have been riding a mule
and dressed in the early nineteenth-century equivalent of a T-shirt, not
a military uniform – the incident is typical of many of the country's
most important political transformations. The decision to break with
the crown was made in complete isolation from the people and
represented the passage of power to a local elite that was no more
interested in democracy than its predecessors were. (A piece of advice
the Emperor had given Pedro a few years before the declaration of

independence would be echoed throughout the country's history: "I fear Brazil might separate itself from Portugal; if so, place the crown on your own head rather than allow it to fall into the hands of an adventurer.")

One pact among the elite, as always consummated to forestall independent interventions by the people, brought about an end to the epoch of slavery. Princess Isabel replaced her father on the throne in 1888 and decreed an end to slavery, thus going down in history as the generous ruler who granted freedom to blacks, and robbing the popular anti-slavery movement of credit for its long campaign. The following year, the republic was proclaimed by a military movement, which deposed the monarchy without popular participation or resistance.

Four decades later, under the impact of the 1929 economic crisis, an army uprising toppled the Luís regime, ushering in fifteen consecutive years of rule by Getúlio Vargas. A leader of the uprising reformulated Dom João's dictate in starker fashion: "We will make the revolution before the people do."

Brazil's two most important political events of the twentieth century – Vargas's rise in 1930 and the military coup d'état in 1964 – both initially manifested ambiguous ideological characteristics, despite the fact that they represented the moments of greatest rupture in the country's history. The political parties that accompanied these events were relatively inconspicuous, passive forces, and proved unable to survive as independent actors for any substantial length of time.

With the 1964 military dictatorship, and especially during the democratic transition process in the 1980s, coherent ideological tendencies began to surface. The PT's birth was one expression of this phenomenon. When the party refused to participate in the (indirectly) military-directed Electoral College vote for president in 1985, denouncing it as a variant of the traditional elite-bartered pacts that would not allow for a complete change of regime, something new was born in Brazil's political history. This refusal to participate in the ruling-class transition, and the public unmasking of its character as the continued tutelage of the old over the new, was quite original in Brazilian politics.

The 1964 coup was conducted in the name of liberalism, against the alleged danger of statism and "communization" represented by the moderately nationalist government of João Goulart, a populist politician linked to former dictator/president Getúlio Vargas. The two basic goals of the military government were the restoration of "social order" and the renewal of economic expansion.

The first was achieved through the systematic repression of all democratic and left forces – from the political parties to the media, universities, and labor movements, and including Congress and the judiciary, which survived largely as a servile extension of state power. The following list of the major repressive acts that followed the declaration of military rule was catalogued by E. Bradford Burns in his excellent book, *A History of Brazil*:

> Fifty-five Congressmen were expelled from the legislature and lost their political rights, thereby increasing the conservative proportion of Congress. Castello Branco (the first military general/president) removed the governors of Amazonas, Pará, Pernambuco, Sergípe, Acre, Rio de Janeiro and Goiás. Former presidents Kubitschek, Quadros, and Goulart were deprived of their political rights for ten years. Approximately 4,500 federal employees lost their jobs. The military ranks were purged and several hundred officers either went into retirement or were dismissed. The hastily created Military Courts of Inquiry summoned more than 9,000 persons to answer charges of corruption or subversion. The Superior Institute of Brazilian Studies was closed, the National Student Union disbanded, labor unions purged, and the Peasant Leagues outlawed.[1]

The military did not immediately do away with the electoral process, but that was soon to come. In late 1965, about eighteen months after the coup, eleven states held gubernatorial elections. Pro-government candidates lost in all but two. That set off a second round of repression, with the powers of the president greatly increased, the end of direct elections for the presidency and the vice-presidency, and the dissolution of all political parties (the generals would soon create ARENA and the MDB to replace the outlawed parties). Four months later, popular elections for governor and mayors of the state capitals were also eliminated. The restrictions did not do away with anti-regime sentiments but went a long way towards silencing them.

The second goal – economic expansion – was accomplished through policies that accelerated the centralization and concentration of capital in the hands of large national and foreign businesses, laying the groundwork for a new era of import substitution (and later export-led growth), responsible for Brazil's period of unprecedented economic expansion from the late 1960s until the end of the following decade.

The years 1968 to 1974 – dubbed the "Economic Miracle" – were especially dynamic, with GNP rising at an average rate of 11.2 per cent annually (industrial output increased even more rapidly, expanding by 15 per cent a year on average). As well as being unprecedented in the country's history such growth was higher than that attained by virtually any country in the world during the period. Not coincidentally, it was accomplished during the time of the most rigorous repression. In December 1968 the infamous Fifth Institutional Act was passed, which temporarily shut down Congress, suspended the constitution and almost all political and civil rights, and further tightened press censorship.

The concentration of income that accompanied this growth was marked, a direct result of the regime's early, and crude, version of "Reaganomics": 75 per cent of the increase in Brazilian income between 1964 and 1974 was appropriated by the richest 10 per cent of the population while the poorest half took in only 10 per cent (between 1960 and 1976, the 80 per cent of the population at the bottom of the social pyramid got poorer, in real terms). A report prepared by the US Overseas Development Council in the mid 1970s gave Brazil a rating of 68 out of a possible 100 on its "Physical Quality of Life Index." That was far below most other Latin countries (Cuba had a rating of 84) and just a notch above the rating of 67 given to one of the region's poorest nations, El Salvador. In 1972, even then president General Emílio Garrastazú Médici was forced to admit, "The economy is going well, the people not so well."[2]

The establishment of the dictatorship was an essential condition for the realization of the goals of "stability" and growth; their attainment subsequently legitimized the regime, first in the eyes of dominant classes and second, after the opposition was defeated and the economic expansion allowed for the fulfillment of consumerist desires, for the middle class as well.

The dictatorship was at the peak of its power. At his 1974 inauguration, General Ernesto Geisel (the third military head of state since 1964, selected by an "electorate" limited to fellow officers) announced that a process of "political opening" (*abertura politica*) would be initiated. The "opening," which Geisel said would be slow and gradual, was a sign not of opposition strength, but of the regime's own confidence that its opponents were thoroughly defeated and conditions for a long period of capitalist expansion securely established.

However, the conditions that had made rapid economic expansion possible were quickly coming to an end, as international capitalism entered a period of worldwide recession beginning in 1974. This hurt Brazilian exports, which were primarily sold to the West. The generals, undeterred, decided to push ahead, while lowering the target for GNP growth to 7 per cent a year, still high by international standards. To do so, the government resorted to greater foreign indebtedness, used largely to finance pharaonic development projects which served as an incentive to private investment.

For years, Brazil had been able to obtain loans easily from private banks and international lenders in order to finance development. This also allowed the country to diversify its trading partners. Though the USA remained the largest single customer, Japan and Western Europe became important clients as well. Thanks to the ready availability of "petrodollars" following the 1973 oil "crisis," lenders were still happy to provide the country with all the money it wanted. (This continued until the early 1980s in fact. By 1980, Brazil's total foreign debt payments represented 259 per cent of total export earnings – 200 per cent was considered the "danger" mark by Morgan Guaranty – yet Brazil was still considered a "five star" borrower.) The strategy soon led to a major increase in the debt and its burden, especially as most loans contracted contained "floating" interest, which rose along with international rates, thus guaranteeing bank profit margins. Between 1974 and 1977, the total debt quadrupled from $12 billion to $50 billion, while $4.2 billion was doled out in interest payments. (By the end of the decade, the "floating interest" loans, initially contracted with interest of 6 to 7 per cent annually, carried rates three times higher due to the increase in international rates caused by tight money policies carried out by the US Federal Reserve during Jimmy Carter's administration. Every time the international rate climbed by one point, Brazil was $1 billion poorer.)

Economic problems created political opposition. In 1974, the year General Geisel took office and announced the political "opening," the MDB obtained its first important electoral success in congressional and state elections. The party nearly doubled its number of federal deputies, from 87 to 165, and tripled its bank of senators from 7 to 21. In total number of votes, the MDB surpassed ARENA, with 14 million to the latter's 10 million. Until that point, the electoral process's lack of legitimacy had compelled the opposition to express itself through the "null vote" or electoral boycotts. With the 1974 results, combined with the defeat of the guerrilla groups which preceded it, most of the political opposition turned to the MDB. Other anti-regime activities were growing as well. In spite of the repression, the student movement began to organize, holding national meetings and carrying out street demonstrations.

There were also some sectors of the local business community who were increasingly disenchanted with the government. Immediately after the coup, the generals had eased rules on the participation of overseas capital in Brazilian industry as well as regulations concerning profit repatriation. The result was a tremendous inflow of direct multinational investment capital and greater participation of foreign firms in Brazilian industry. Large numbers of local entrepreneurs were forced into bankruptcy. By 1971, key sectors of the economy such as automobiles, machinery, mining and rubber were dominated by foreign firms. The same year the American magazine *Business Week* was enthusiastically telling its readers that profit opportunities in Brazil were just about the best in the world.[3]

Despite the military's strong anti-communism, the generals built up a powerful state sector as well, further reducing areas of the economy available for exploitation by national business. American political scientist Peter Evans described Brazil's economic base in the late 1970s as one formed by a "Triple Alliance," with multinational, state, and local capital all having assigned roles. The latter, in Evans's view, was a sort of junior partner, though it still played a significant role in promoting development. (Evans dubbed the overall economic model as one of "dependent development," due to its intricate ties with international capitalism, in terms of direct investment, foreign loans and markets for exports.[4])

The business community's complaints, then, centered around the denationalization and debilitation of local industry, but its leaders' public complaints focused on the lack of democracy. In late 1977, several thousand business officials met in Rio and called on the regime to restore civil liberties; a short time later eight major industrialists signed a statement urging a more just distribution of wealth.[5]

But it was the resurgence of labor that would transform the nature of the political opposition. The intensification of the industrialization process strengthened the working class, especially that segment concentrated on the periphery of São Paulo, the country's largest economic center. Class-based tendencies in the union movement, supported by the Roman Catholic Church, emerged, most importantly in the automobile industry (which included such foreign giants as Ford,

Chrysler and Volkswagen). In 1978, the government was shaken when the first strike in a decade was called by metalworkers in São Paulo. This marked the start of an unending cycle of conflicts between labor on one side and the state and capital on the other. A new generation of union activists emerged during this period and they would command the most important mobilizations of the decade, with strikes that challenged, and finally broke, the draconian wage policy of the military regime. Union leaders received national support in their battles with the government, and for the first time ever the working class would occupy center stage of the country's political scene.

As the regime's opponents gained strength, the political opening process changed course. In 1979, Geisel handed the presidency over to General João Figueiredo. Liberalization continued, but the regime, under the pressure of a negative international situation, climbing inflation, and an emboldened political and social opposition, had been seriously weakened. Among Figueiredo's first moves was to decree an end to the principal acts of political exclusion imposed by his predecessors. Thousands of exiles banished in the years following the coup were allowed to return home, political prisoners were released, the law prohibiting the formation of new political parties was revoked, press censorship was loosened, the powers of the military government were diminished and an electoral calendar was established calling for the direct election of state governors in 1982. However, an indirect presidential ballot, to be conducted in 1984 by an Electoral College composed of the National Congress, was maintained.

The ideological concept guiding these operations was "decompression," a popular theory among Western elite planners at precisely this time. The theory had been formulated by North American Yale University Professor Samuel Huntington of the Trilateral Commission, and its central proposition was that capitalism could not withstand the demands placed upon it by liberal democracy. Therefore, governments needed to filter and control demands made by popular sectors of society (the poor, blacks, environmentalists, feminists, and so on). In Brazil, this theory was embodied in the armed forces' idea of "tutored democracy." General Geisel, when announcing the liberalization, had said it would be "slow and gradual," provided state control proved able to channel the process. By 1978, that control had been considerably weakened due to the slowdown in economic expansion and the renewed surge of anti-government sentiment.

With Figueiredo's decree of more liberal laws pertaining to the rights of the legal opposition, especially the 1979 party reform bill, a new party structure emerged. The MDB changed its name to the Brazilian Democratic Movement Party (PMDB), and continued to encompass a broad sector of the opposition, but maintained its liberal hegemony. However, the main transformation was the rise of an opposition front of ideologically defined left-wing parties. Fernando Henrique Cardoso, a politician and prominent left-center sociologist, characterized the PMDB as an "omnibus" party, one which encompassed extremely diverse sectors. Cardoso, himself a member of the PMDB, contrasted this type of party with "ideological" ones – with specific programs, strategies and tactics – which he considered too rigid for the democratic transformation that Brazilian society was undergoing.

The new ideological parties Cardoso was criticizing included the PT and the Democratic Labor Party (PDT), organized by the ex-governor of Rio Grande do Sul, Leonel Brizola, a populist leader who defended the ideas of Getúlio Vargas and João Goulart, Brizola's brother-in-law. Later, the two surviving communist factions also formed parties, one linked to the USSR and the other espousing Maoism (the Brazilian Communist Party and the Communist Party of Brazil, respectively).

The debut of the new party structure took place with the gubernatorial and congressional elections of late 1982. The electoral climate was favorable to the opposition, with an economic recession unfolding, in great part created by the increasing burden of debt servicing. For the first time since official statistics were kept in the post-war period, Brazil's economy was registering negative growth. This was the start of what came to be known throughout Latin America as the "lost decade," with living standards plunging almost everywhere and most countries coming under the tutelage of the foreign debt and financial capital.

The electoral results were a huge triumph for the opposition, especially the PMDB, which did well in the more industrialized south and urban centers. The PMDB elected governors in São Paulo and Minas Gerais and, for the first time since the military coup, controlled a majority in Congress. (Brizola won the governor's race in Rio de Janeiro, despite an attempt to cheat him out of victory by rigging the vote-counting process.) The PMDB emerged from the balloting as a great national party, representing a continuation of the broad-based, ideologically amorphous opposition which had developed during the previous decade. The pro-government Social Democratic Party (PDS), which had replaced ARENA with the 1979 reform law, was left confined to the impoverished north and northeast, where it managed to elect most of the governors and a large bank of state and national congressional representatives.

After the vote, attention shifted to the Electoral College presidential election scheduled for two years down the road. The opposition unleashed a national campaign for direct elections, whose leaders included PMDB president Ulysses Guimarães and the PT's Lula. Huge rallies were held throughout the country and the campaign, dubbed "Diretas Já!" ("Direct Elections Now!"), became the largest political mass movement Brazil had ever known. In 1984 a huge rally in São Paulo was the largest and most remarkable political rally the country had seen (and would be surpassed in size and emotion, only during Lula's 1989 presidential campaign). PMDB leader Cardoso later described events leading up to the rally and the event itself:

No one imagined what would happen with the campaign for direct elections. . . . In December [of 1983], Ulysses met in Brasília [with party officials] and proposed a schedule of debates about a direct election, because he planned on traveling throughout the country during the holidays. We wanted to have some rallies, but if that wasn't possible we'd hold meetings in closed quarters. Then, there was Alfonsín's inauguration in Argentina and the vision of holding huge rallies excited [the opposition]. [Franco] Montoro went and returned extremely excited, he called Ulysses and me and he wanted to schedule a rally. I called together the executive committee of the party . . . and everyone, without exception, thought it unwise to do so. Everyone thought it was risky, even the PT and the PDT.

We were very anxious because we thought it was extremely bold to hold a rally in the Praça da Sé [a major square in front of the city's main church]. No one had ever filled the Praça da Sé. I, who am very prudent in my estimates, thought we'd have 20,000, 30,000 people, which would have been enormous by our calculations. And 300,000 came! . . . When I arrived, the emotion was indescribable. To see all those people! It started to rain but no one left. . . . The sound system was terrible and half the people there couldn't hear anything, and the speeches were far from brilliant. The people were there not to hear their leaders, but to show their noncomformity.[6]

The "Diretas Já!" campaign helped establish a social and political consensus that the people had the right to choose the president of the republic. To achieve this objective, though, the military-drafted constitution had to be amended, which required a two-thirds vote of Congress. Despite the backing of a group of deputies and senators who abandoned the military regime as its boat was sinking, the amendment failed by 22 votes (approval required 320 out of 479 votes; the opposition got 298). Thus, the Electoral College voting system was maintained. However, the opposition, as demonstrated by the vote on the amendment for direct elections, already had a majority in Congress. That majority became more comfortable when many of the government's long-time supporters ditched the military PDS to form the Liberal Front Party (PFL). They allied themselves with the PMDB, creating the "Democratic Alliance," and selected Tancredo Neves, a moderate ex-governor of Minas Gerais state who participated marginally in the popular campaign for direct elections, to be their candidate in the upcoming Electoral College vote. The former head of the PDS, Senator José Sarney – a representative of the traditional rural northeastern oligarchy and one of the leaders of the campaign against direct elections – was named Neves's vice presidential candidate. It was widely believed that Sarney was put on the ticket at the behest of the military, as a quid pro quo for allowing an opposition victory.

Neves's rival for the presidency was ex-São Paulo state governor Paulo Maluf, a prototypical representative of the old regime whose reputation for corruption and clientelism embodied the worst characteristics of political life under the dictatorship. A consensus against his candidacy soon formed, which benefited the Neves/Sarney ticket and also facilitated the swift passage of many long-time regime hacks into the opposition camp, simply to oppose the repudiated candidacy of Maluf. Anti-Malufism thus became a fragile, and misleading, dividing line between "liberals" and "authoritarians."

Neves won a comfortable victory in the Electoral College vote. The only party which refused to participate was the PT, since it considered the College an authoritarian tool to head off a popular vote and, hence, spurious and illegitimate. Neves, the traditional Brazilian politician par excellence, was thought to have a good chance of reconciling the antagonistic positions of the opposition and expanding the ideological spectrum of the Democratic Alliance. He formed a ministry that combined long-standing members of the opposition with politicians who had only recently abandoned the dictatorship, as well as moderate technocrats. But in an incident that surely ranks among the most

bizarre in Brazilian political history (alongside Getúlio Vargas's suicide in 1954 and Janio Quadros's resignation in 1961 after having
occupied the presidency for only seven months – he cited "occult
forces"), Neves fell ill on the very eve of his inauguration and was
rushed to a Brasília hospital for emergency surgery. The inaugural
ceremony of Brazil's first civilian president since the 1964 coup proved
to be an anti-climax: instead of Neves, the green-and-yellow presidential sash was passed to Sarney, who had resigned his position as PDS
president just weeks earlier.

Meanwhile, the country's attention was focused on the hospital bed
where Neves lay. Officials attempted to transmit confidence to the
astonished population, many of whom believed Neves's illness
resulted from a plot to frustrate the democratic transition. But his
health worsened dramatically, despite the efforts of a huge team of
doctors. (Later, when Neves's irreversible decline was impossible to
hide, it was learned that he had developed an infection during the
emergency surgery he underwent the night before his scheduled
inauguration, due to the large number of people in the room at the
time.)

Two months later, when Neves died, the country was immersed in
a state of political "continuismo" deeper than anything even the most
cynical had expected. An illusory hope existed that Sarney, who was
sorely lacking in both legitimacy and credibility, would commit
himself to democratic reforms more profound than Neves had proposed, in an attempt to buttress his very limited popular support. That
hope was not realized. Soon after promising a major agrarian reform
program (announced at a gathering of rural workers, to heighten his
supposed commitment to the issue), Sarney backtracked, pressured by
the rural oligarchy and the conservative press. That move was typical
of the vacillation and political weakness demonstrated during his
entire period in power.

After floundering for most of his first year in office, in February
1986 Sarney launched the "Cruzado Plan," an emergency economic
program named after the new national currency it created. The plan,
modeled on an anti-inflationary program instituted by the Raúl Alfonsín government in neighboring Argentina, was implemented to control skyrocketing inflation, and represented the Sarney government's
best chance of legitimizing the ongoing conservative transition. In
addition to the new currency, the Cruzado Plan implemented a wage
and price freeze, and attempted to channel resources from the financial

to the productive sector. Initial popular support was overwhelming. The price freeze lowed inflation from an annual level approaching 300 per cent to the low double-digits and the economy grew at a rate of around 10 per cent. Housewives became "Sarney's watchdogs," and monitored prices at supermarkets. Those who failed to abide by the price freeze found themselves the target of popular protests, and even sackings. For the first time, citizens enjoyed the power to influence an economic process that had seemed permanently out of control.

The economy's rapid growth produced significant gains for almost all sectors of the population, and led to a consumer spending spree which, though largely confined to the middle class, benefited the poor as well. Merchandise destined for export was redirected towards the internal market, and for a while appeared on supermarket shelves. Partly as a result, the country's trade surplus plunged (from $1.3 billion in May 1986 to only $136 million in March 1987), making it increasingly difficult for the government to make payments on the foreign debt (and demonstrating one important barrier to implementing redistributive economic policies without addressing the debt problem).

The plan's success was only temporary, however. Producers sabotaged the price freeze by withholding goods from the market as a means of obtaining price increases; and financial capital, which was not hit directly by the plan, soon recovered and was able to make hefty profits via the time-honored tradition of financial speculation. Sarney, who briefly enjoyed the highest approval ratings of any Brazilian president since nationwide polling began, refused to deepen the economic or social reforms which would have been necessary to ensure the success of the program. Less than a year after the announcement of the Cruzado Plan, inflation returned with a vengeance, and Sarney's support plummeted.

Important elections were held in November, though, while the plan was still popular, and the results were crucial to the country's future. In addition to governors' races in all states, the Congress elected was to prepare a civilian constitution to replace the military's 1967 charter. The government's allies campaigned on their support of the Cruzado Plan – even as the president, who was made an honorary member of the PMDB to help the party in the elections, was quietly preparing to scrap it. Opposition parties, meanwhile, found campaigning difficult, as pro-government candidates basked in the glory of the Cruzado Plan, which appeared to have laid the groundwork for a long period of low-inflation economic growth. When the votes came in, the PMDB had won 22 of 23 state governorships and an absolute majority in the House and Senate. The PFL won the final governor's post, in the northeastern state of Sergipe, and the second largest number of seats in both houses of Congress, and thus, the Constituent Assembly.

Then, in an amazingly cynical move, even by the shameful standards of Brazil's political elite, the Cruzado Plan's price freeze was ditched even before all the votes had come in (it took about a week to count all the ballots). The move provoked a flood of phone calls to electoral centers with outraged citizens asking if it was too late to change their votes. By then, of course, it was too late; the government had won the battle, even if the move would ultimately cost it the war, as well as serve to discredit civilian rule in the minds of many.

When the Cruzado Plan was fully dismantled a short time later, and the economy was again heading towards chaos, popular expectations received their third significant blow in a very short period of time. First came the failure of the direct elections movement, then Neves's death, and, perhaps the greatest blow of all, the collapse of the anti-inflationary plan. Its failure produced an outburst of cynicism (car bumperstickers popular during the plan's heyday read, "I Believe"; they were soon replaced by ones reading "I Believed") that had long-term implications for the future of Brazilian democracy.

Just two years after Sarney had taken office, his government seemed all too familiar, if not in its repressive aspect, at least in its representation of the privileged faction of the dominant class, its reliance on traditional politicians of the old regime and the same oligarchic style of rule. When the new Congress, acting as a Constituent Assembly, first met in early 1987 the country was governed by an essentially hybrid political regime: a mixture of institutional structures surviving from the previous regime and innovations introduced during the ongoing conservative-led transition to civilian rule.

The democratic transition had as its point of departure a regime with well-defined characteristics: a military dictatorship which put into practice policies predominantly favorable to large foreign and domestic capital. Within this regime, the armed forces played the protagonist's role, allied with technocrats linked to the economic interests that provided the government's principal base of support. The ideology of national security, which identified social conflicts and political contradictions as resulting from a foreign virus – "communist subversion" – permeated all acts of the dictatorship. And, crucially, the generals were able to negotiate their exit from government: the regime did not collapse, as had been the case in Argentina following the junta's disastrous attempt to retake the Malvinas Islands.

With the inauguration of Sarney, the military dictatorship as a political regime ceased to exist. Political power would henceforth be mediated by a Congress with reinforced powers, and the right to political organization was broadened, as was the liberty of the mass media. High-ranking armed forces officials withdrew from the political scene, becoming more discreet actors. Political prisoners were freed, security organs had reduced roles, judicial guarantees were obtained and put into effect.

A theory frequently cited by PMDB intellectuals in explaining – and justifying – the transition process was so-called "Authoritarianism Theory," originally developed by Spanish sociologist Juan Linz as an explanation of the end of Franco's rule. In accordance with this theory, the Brazilian military government was only a more flexible variant of a regime of "exclusion," when an opposition was tolerated and political and economic hegemony – in a diffused manner in Brazil – was in the hands of the "state bourgeoisie."

This type of regime resulted from an enormous concentration of wealth and power in the hands of technocrats, who slowly became a class in themselves. Within this regime, the theory goes, national and foreign capital would be absolved of responsibility, in that they favored a free market economy and interlocutors more receptive to their interests. A broad opposition front was a logical, and necessary, consequence of such a regime, formed of diverse sectors ranging from large-scale financial and industrial capital to class-based unions, which would challenge the state bourgeoisie and its authoritarian regime. The natural objective of such a front, said Linz, was the establishment of a "state of law" based on liberal institutions, with a separation of the three branches of state power and the affirmation of an autonomous civil society.

Linz's theory of authoritarianism became the ideology of the conservative transition. The economic and social constraints that prevented the great majority of the population from exercising full citizenship rights were conveniently overlooked; once the basic principles of liberal democracy were established, moderate opposition leaders said, the democratic transition would be complete. However, economic and military checks on democracy would clearly still remain, and they did.

The economic limitations resulted from the process of capital accumulation associated with the military regime, especially its debt-based nature. Maintaining high levels of economic expansion based on foreign indebtedness was a time-bomb, sure to explode at a later date. The equally problematic internal debt was largely a byproduct of the foreign situation, since the government used state-owned enterprises to contract foreign loans. The resulting indebtedness of these firms obliged the government to issue short-term bonds to finance the ensuing public sector deficit, thus helping create the speculative financial spiral that has plagued the country every since.

The foreign and domestic debts created the minefield on which the Brazilian democratic transition would take place. By the early 1980s, Brazil was paying out over 10 per cent of the total debt annually in interest payments alone (it stopped paying principal in 1983), without reducing the existing mountain of debt. The country's entire trade surplus, which grew throughout the 1980s (trailing only those of Japan and West Germany by the end of the decade, when it was about $15 billion annually), went to pay off debt, instead of being invested in infrastructure and other productive areas. This drainage of resources makes the extension of full citizenship rights to the bulk of the population impossible, as the money needed to finance social reform is leaving the country.

At the same time, the transition process never confronted the question of the demilitarization of Brazilian society. The armed forces were no longer the backbone of the political system, with high-ranking officers the fundamental source of government decision-making, but the military continued to cast a long shadow on the Brazilian state. During the Sarney years, the military controlled five cabinet-level positions; one for each head of the three branches of the armed forces, one for the head of the National Intelligence Service (a sort of combined FBI-CIA, later renamed by Collor but which continued to spy on the population), and one for the military chief of staff. Other military officials continued to hold key posts at lower, but crucial, levels of power; for example, the armed forces fully controlled nuclear energy and research programs and exercised great influence on all planning in regard to the Amazon. The military maintained a significant presence in state-owned enterprises as well, and ministers still felt free to make political proclamations to the press, especially at times of crises (thus reminding civilian leaders of the generals' continued influence). The new civilian constitution itself, promulgated in 1988, reserves to the armed forces the right to intervene in internal affairs, as long as they are called upon by one of the branches of government to preserve "law and order."

Military and financial tutelage served as a bridge between the old and the new regime, linking them in a reformulated continuity of past and present: the hegemony of monopoly and financial capital, both foreign and domestic, was guaranteed as long as financial tutelage – made concrete in the form of the domestic and foreign debt – remained unbroken. The military presence, on the other hand, continued as a barrier against a full state of law and full civilian control over the government.

Twenty-five years of military dictatorship and unelected leadership had left a highly centralized society in terms of wealth and power and an extremely divided one socially. Despite a negative economic picture overall – or perhaps because of it – capital accumulation expanded comfortably during the 1980s. Banks and financial institutions made record profits, while industrial and agricultural producers found in the external market an outlet for their products, in compensation for declining sales at home. Large construction firms continued to receive huge contracts from the state, and also expanded their operations overseas. The rich had more top-quality products to choose from than ever before, as evidenced by the increasing availability of sophisticated electronic and computer products as well as the growing domestic production of luxury automobiles (and the decline of cheaper models favored by the middle class).

Business profits did not translate into economic stability, however. By the end of the 1980s, inflation had risen from about 100 per cent at the start of the decade to well over 1,000 per cent annually at the end, and this was the country's main problem. Incessant inflation ate up workers' buying power, disorganized the pricing system (prices charged by industry and retail outlets for their products were rarely based on costs; instead, when the previous month's inflation figure was announced, they simply jacked up their prices by the same amount, or a little more), and led to a declining rate of internal investment (falling from 23 per cent of GNP in 1981 to 17.2 per cent in 1989). With high inflation and even higher interest rates (necessary to attract investors to finance the internal debt), firms found it even more profitable to use their resources to buy short-term high-paying financial bonds, dollars and gold; by the end of the decade an estimated $20 billion was tied up in speculation.

Further dampening economic growth was the unending problem of the foreign debt. Despite the fact that Brazil was an exporter of capital to the First World, remitting more in loan payments than it received in new money and foreign investment (the latter amounted to just $400 million in the final year of the decade, less than a quarter of its 1981 total), the debt continued to grow until it reached about $115 billion in 1989. This contributed to the almost total incapacity of the state to direct economic growth and attempt to promote development.

The general picture by the decade's end was grim: the country's GNP, which grew by an average of 6.1 per cent in the 1970s, slowed to a rate of 2.9 per cent in the 1980s (virtually no growth at all in terms of per capita GNP). Behind the numbers, a huge social crisis had emerged. The economic model – which promoted income concentration, excluded the majority from the consumption market, and created a huge reserve army of labor – was completely incompatible with any type of social equilibrium. The agricultural sector, dominated by large-scale producers, was especially problematic; while the production of basic foodstuffs for the internal market lagged behind needs, millions of poor Brazilians were forced off the land and had no choice but to emigrate to urban areas, where conditions of health, housing, employment, education and transportation were so lacking that the reproduction of poverty was inevitable. While half of all the country's poor remain in the interior, the other half now lives on the periphery of the great urban centers, especially São Paulo and Rio, in the slums and the tenements.

The scale of the economic, social and political crisis that Brazil faced at the end of the 1980s altered the national consciousness from one of confidence to one of disbelief in the country's capacity to overcome its difficulties. An old joke seemed more apt than ever: "Brazil is the country of the future. And it always will be."

However, beneath the surface the social transformations wrought by the development process had created the basis for a challenging of the status quo. Though the society that emerged from the period of military and unelected rule had an intricate network of covert and overt types of social control, economic misery and grassroots political organizing led a greater and greater share of the population to question the system's ideological and institutional underpinnings. The PT's birth in the late 1970s helped hasten and intensify that process.

NOTES

1. E. Bradford Burns, *A History of Brazil*, Columbia University Press, p. 510.
2. Ibid., p. 534
3. Ibid., p. 530. Perhaps knowing that the generals would encourage overseas investment, US president Lyndon Johnson had sent down an aircraft carrier, half a dozen destroyers, and a pile of ammunition to show support for the coup. The USA immediately recognized the new government and rushed down economic aid. The full extent of American involvement in the coup is still not clear, but it is known that US officials were well aware that a plot against the Goulart government was unfolding and in no way discouraged its planners. The evidence is that American involvement went well beyond that.
4. Peter Evans, *Dependent Development: The Alliance of Multinational, State and Local Capital in Brazil*, Princeton University Press.
5. Burns, p. 525.
6. Interview in *Playboy*, September 1984, p. 117.

3

The São Paulo Strikes
and the Birth of the PT

When I remember how the average São Bernardo worker thought ten years ago and [compare it with] the way he thinks today, I realize my struggle may have been tiring, but it was worth it.

Lula, September, 1989.

She cried when I was able to get a job as a metalworker. Imagine if she could see me now.

Lula, November, 1989, after winning a place in the presidential election runoff, talking about his mother, who had died in 1980

When discussing his personal history, PT leader Luís Inácio Lula da Silva recalls he was an "apolitical" union activist in the early 1970s. He was not alone. With the military regime having banned and repressed almost all types of independent political activity, and the economy still booming, the generals had largely succeeded in quieting opposition to their rule. Unions continued to form but were tightly controlled. The major benefits workers received were simply paternalistic handouts and services, such as medical examination and even haircuts. Furthermore, most labor leaders were docile lapdogs, abandoning political demands and meekly accepting the government's wage policy.

The only real political organizing that took place at the time was under the umbrella of the country's powerful Roman Catholic Church. While the Church had initially backed the coup, by the late 1960s prominent bishops and priests began openly criticizing the regime's repression and economic policies.

One of the earliest and most important Church leaders to confront the generals was Cardinal Paulo Evaristo Arns of São Paulo. A short, soft-spoken Franciscan, Arns was initially considered a member of the clergy's conservative wing. At the time of the coup, he was a theology professor in a seminary near Rio and made special trips by jeep to offer counseling to army troops.

Like many of his Latin American colleagues – including Archbishop Oscar Romero of El Salvador, murdered by that country's death squads – Arns's views changed as he witnessed the practical effects of dictatorship: a crucial turning point in his political journey took place when a worker's child died in his arms. As he said, in discussing his increasingly critical views of the generals' policies, "The [military] government says its most important concern is for people, but what we see is the opposite: its most important concern is for profits." Arns was just as outspoken in his condemnation of torture and his defence of political prisoners. Absolutely fearless, he would personally go to army bases and jails to demand information about prisoners. His persistence was such that the military was once forced to replace an important São Paulo army commander who reportedly was involved in the torture of government "enemies."[1]

Arns's leadership cannot be overestimated. His São Paulo archdiocese became a symbol of resistance, due to his denunciation of torture and repression, and his strong support for working-class organizations and actions. As described by Jane Kramer, in the *New Yorker*:

> Masses at the cathedral in São Paulo . . . became a kind of high theatre of resistance. Thousands of people came to them. The army would send troops to shoot the mourners – the official word was "terrorists" – and the troops would wait for the Mass to end, their rifles pointed at the cathedral door; but when the doors opened hundreds of priests and nuns would be scattered among the mourners, dressed in ordinary street clothes, and there was no way to tell them apart. "Inverting the pyramid," Cardinal Arns called it, because what the Catholic soldiers saw, standing on the cathedral steps and singing the "canto final," was the whole community of their church, defying them to fire. It was an exercise in passive resistance of great cunning and simplicity, and it was repeated in churches all over Latin America.[2]

While many Church leaders still backed the military, discreetly or otherwise, increasing numbers joined Arns in offering support for the opposition, especially the poor. (Another key Church figure was Bishop Helder Camara of the northeastern city of Recife. He received numerous death threats due to his attacks on the government and the generals banned his name from even being mentioned – positively or negatively – in the news media.) This helped prevent the generals from completely closing the door on civil society and kept alive the flickering remains of independent organization, yet despite the efforts of these leaders, the generals felt secure in their total control of the political scene.

Crucial to that control was the longstanding weakness of the union movement, which had been institutionalized in 1942 when the Vargas regime passed the Consolidation of Brazilian Labor Law (CLT). Under the law (which has now been greatly modified, though still retaining some repressive aspects), unions were considered legal only after being authorized by the Labor Ministry – thus recognition depended on the government, not the companies with which workers negotiated. The Ministry collected an annual trade union tax, the equivalent of one day's wage per worker, and the money was used to run the whole system, with 80 per cent going to unions (and their national and regional federations) and the rest remaining with the state. Each union had its share of the funds kept in the Banco do Brasil, but the money could be frozen if CLT regulations were broken. The Labor Minister was also authorized to remove labor leaders from office and shut down unions. Finally, the government, through the Labor Courts, would rule strikes illegal.

Another feature of the CLT that stunted labor was the stipulation that individual unions represent workers of a given profession in one county only. In order to gain governmental recognition, a third of all county workers from an occupational category were required to sign cards endorsing the union. This was especially hard in some rural areas where City Hall simply would not provide the total number of workers, or would wildly inflate figures so that one-third quota was impossible to obtain. Also, if two different groups were attempting to organize the same category, the Labor Ministry was always free to select the one it felt was less likely to cause trouble.

Even though union organizing was proliferating at the time of the 1964 coup, the labor movement was still a marginal player. Unions had finally reached the interior, but in very small numbers, and only a few million urban workers were organized. While unions were not outlawed by the generals, the dictatorship launched a sharp crackdown soon after taking power. During their first six years in power, the Labor Minister used CLT regulations to intervene in 536 local, state and regional labor organizations (80 per cent of these actions took place during the regime's first two years in power). Over a hundred union activists and their congressional supporters were stripped of their political rights during the same period. Three illegal strikes were called by industrial workers in 1968, two in Minas Gerais state and the other in Osasco, São Paulo. The government immediately repressed the actions with brutal police force, and succeeded in breaking the back of labor opposition to the dictatorship. For virtually the next decade, unions rarely challenged the regime, either on ideological or financial grounds.[3]

Much of the union movement's conservatism resulted less from its leaders' explicit backing of the regime's goals than from the fact that the labor bureaucracy established by the CLT provided thousands of sinecures. One observer explained that mainstream union leaders had a vested interest in maintaining the status quo as the system "permitted an immense contingent of officials spread among the 4,672 unions, 159 federations and 21 confederations to have a modest, but assured career."[4]

Rapid economic growth, extreme income inequality, and the development of an urban pole of highly sophisticated industries in São Paulo laid the groundwork for the reemergence of radical unionism. It was in the mid 1970s, due to a combination of the regime's political liberalization and a new generation of union militants willing to confront the dictatorship, that labor took its place at center stage.

The militant unionists that emerged during the 1970s were dubbed the "authentics," and were mostly based in São Paulo state. In addition to Lula, they included Benedito Marcilio from the Santo Andrade metalworkers; Henos Amorina, a leader of the metalworkers in Osasco; Paulo de Mattos Skromov, from the city's leatherworkers; Jaco Bittar, president of the militant oilworkers union in Campinas; Benedito Marcilio and José Cicotte from the Santo Andrade metalworkers; Hugo Perez of the São Paulo electric workers; and metalworkers' leader Arnaldo Gonçalves from the port city of Santos. From outside the state came Olivio Dutra, a bankworkers' union leader in the southern capital of Porto Alegre, and Wagner Benevides from the oilworkers' union in Minas Gerais.

Their early demands, in addition to a return of democratic rule, were a complete overhaul of existing labor legislation, with new rules to include:

• Direct contract negotiations between labor and business. Workers at the time were granted wage increases only by the Labor Court, whose judges were normally reliable regime hacks. Also, pay rises were given only once per year; as inflation picked up throughout most of the 1970s, workers' wages bought far less at the end of the year than they had twelve months earlier. As a result, real purchasing power was forever dropping, even during the 1968–1974 "economic miracle." That, of course, was central to the military's wage policy.

• The organization of union committees on shop floors, and recognition of union delegations.
• Union autonomy from the Labor Ministry.
• The unrestricted right to strike.[5]

Most of the "authentics" later helped found the Central Workers Union (CUT), the radical left labor federation, in 1983. The conservative labor leaders who opposed the "authentics" generally had close ties to the PC and the MDB. These unionists later founded the General Confederation of Workers (CGT), which has preached the "unionism of results" – in short, more money – and which has as its model the American AFL–CIO.

Lula, whose personal background was integral to his success as a union and political leader, played a crucial role in labor's early stirrings. Born in 1945 in the impoverished northeastern town of Garanhuns, Pernambuco, Lula was the youngest of eight brothers born to Aristides and Euridice da Silva. His family eked out a living as subsistence farmers but just weeks after Lula was born, his father moved to the southern port of Santos, forty-five miles from São Paulo. Seven years later, the rest of the family piled on to the back of a truck and also headed for Santos, a trip that lasted thirteen days. It was a journey similar to that taken by an estimated 24 million Brazilians in the past forty years, who fled the northeast in search of better living conditions in the more developed south – one of the great mass migrations in human history. When Lula's family arrived in Santos, they discovered that Aristides had another wife – his mother's cousin – and four children.

Like many other migrants, the da Silvas found life in the south a struggle. The family stayed in Santos for four years, where Lula went to school and helped supplement the family's income by selling peanuts and candies on the street. He also learned to read at the age of ten, when his mother insisted he enrol in a nearby school.

In 1956, the family moved to São Paulo, where they lived in a small room in the back of a bar, and shared a bathroom with the customers. At the time, Lula was not interested in politics, and like millions of boys in soccer-crazy Brazil, he dreamed of a career as a professional player.[6] He remembers that his only awareness of social inequality was being embarrassed by not having a single chair to offer his guests.[7].

In São Paulo, Lula was forced to drop out of school and worked as an office boy and then at a dry cleaners, before finally landing a job at the age of thirteen in a factory that manufactured nuts and bolts. This was considered a major achievement for someone from his background. On his first day on the job, he ran home in his work overalls, his hands deliberately dirtied, to show off to his mother. Work shifts at the plant stretched from 7 a.m. to 7 p.m., and safety standards were almost non-existent; this led to an accident in which Lula lost the little finger on his left hand.

In 1963, Lula got a new job at Industrias Villares, a unionized capital-goods producer in São Bernardo do Campo, an industrial suburb on the outskirts of São Paulo and home to most of Brazil's foreign-owned automobile manufacturers. (The industrialized region outside São Paulo is popularly known as the ABCD, for the four most important cities: Santo Andrade, São Bernardo do Campo, São Caetano do Sul and Diadema.) But it was not until four years later – three years after the military coup – that he bothered going to the union office, and even then it was only at the insistence of his older brother, José Ferreira da Silva, a militant with the then clandestine Brazilian Communist Party.

Lula remembers that he had long thought labor groups were harmful to workers' interests, and desperately avoided talking to his brother about the subject: "All the rest of my family was anti-union, we thought . . . that they were only thieves, that all the leaders were crooks . . . and that my brother was crazy to belong to the union. This was the source of a permanent fight. . . . We'd have a family meeting or we'd be drinking cachaça, and there he'd be: 'because the union . . .' And as soon as he'd start, everyone would be against him . . . because we didn't want to hear about it."[8]

But Lula, who had to be dragged into labor activism, quickly became one of the union's most important members: in 1972, he won a seat on the São Bernardo Metalworkers Union's directory board. (The same year he married his second wife, Marisa Leticia, the widow of a slain taxi driver. Lula was also a widower; his first wife, Maria de Lourdes, died of hepatitis a few months after their wedding in 1969.)

Three years later, he was elected union president with 92 per cent of the vote from the 140,000-strong membership. Oddly enough, Lula was nominated for the presidency by outgoing union head Paulo Vidal, an ideological opponent who he suspected had far from innocent motives: "I had never spoken at a union assembly, had never used a microphone, so – and this is a supposition – when Paulo agreed to nominate me he had the objective of proving, not just for the directorate but for the category as well, that he was irreplaceable. That I was a shit, and couldn't get a damn thing done."[9]

Coinciding with Lula's election was a renewed surge of opposition activities. In addition to the Church, groups such as the Brazilian Bar Association had stepped up their attacks on the government, as the generals showed no interest in a return to democracy and their economic policies were clearly increasing social inequalities.

Lula remembers that he was "apolitical" at the time, and had a very limited vision of his role as a labor organizer. A key turning point came the year he was elected union president, when he traveled to Japan at the invitation of labor leaders there. During the trip, his older brother, Jośe Ferreira, was arrested on charges of being a communist "subversive." Lula said his arrest "was a preponderant factor in my losing all the inhibitions I had. I was a common union leader, I was afraid of being arrested, I worried about my family, I had never thought being a union activist required very much. After my brother was arrested, I lost the fear. . . . It was good because it woke in me a very strong class consciousness."[10]

(Lula learned of his brother's arrest during a brief stopover in the United States after the conference in Japan. He was advised by a labor lawyer that he might be better off staying in the USA for a while, but told him, "Look my friend, the situation is the following; I don't speak the language of these guys here, I've got no money, the food stinks, there's no rice, no beans. I'd rather be arrested in Brazil than stay in this dump of a country."[11])

The first signs of increasing labor militance came in 1976, when, for the first time ever Lula's São Bernardo union was able to make gains in the Labor Court system, winning a small wage rise, job stability for pregnant workers, and a few other minor demands. (Ironically, Lula and other young leaders at first received relatively friendly treatment from the tightly controlled media, as they were not tied to banned communist groups.)

Things heated up a year later. With the economic situation worsening, and production in the automobile industry down, the companies began laying workers off, and substituting long-serving, highly paid workers with new hires who were paid far less.[12] The final straw came when a secret World Bank report was leaked to the press, which showed the government had been manipulating the official measure of inflation. While the dictatorship had claimed the cost of living rose 14.9 per cent in 1973, the report showed the real figure was 22.5 per cent. That lie had resulted in a 34.1 per cent real salary loss for workers between 1973 and 1974, and the São Bernardo Metalworkers Union immediately began a campaign to recuperate that loss. Though the union was unable to get the government to give ground on the issue, the mobilization that resulted laid the groundwork for the huge labor conflicts that followed. As Lula recalled later, "1977 was a year in which various sectors of society screamed out to find a little bit of oxygen, to breathe a little more. Everyone complained, including the workers. But the workers didn't publicly protest. A number of times we were called to take part in other movements but we were always suspicious, worrying about getting involved in something that wasn't directly related to workers. But we also had the consciousness that if the workers didn't speak out, nothing new would happen in the country."[13]

The explosion was soon to come. The opening shot was fired in 1978 by the São Bernardo union, where Lula led a strike at the Saab-Scania truck company. This was Brazil's first large-scale strike in a decade – and it was also the first time Lula ever spoke to a strike assembly. The union demanded a 20 per cent pay rise (above inflation) and the right to negotiate directly with the company, without the interference of the government or the labor courts. On the first day of the strike, workers showed up for their scheduled shifts and clocked in, but refused to start their machines. The movement soon spread to other plants, owned by multinational giants such as Ford, Mercedes, Volkswagen and Chrysler, with some 80,000 workers conducting sit-down strikes by the end of the second week.

The strike took the government completely by surprise, and the military failed to repress the action. Thus, the automakers were forced to negotiate with the strikers, and ended up conceding a 24.5 per cent pay rise on May 31. As Lula pointed out at the time, "The great victory, even more than the wage increase, was that we forced the companies to negotiate an agreement directly with the union, without government interference."[14] With the metalworkers paving the way, other strikes soon erupted in a number of other industries in various regions of the country. By the end of the year, over half a million workers were on strike in six states, as well as the capital city of Brasília, the Federal District. Many won pay rises above those that had been authorized by the government. These victories were the first nails in the coffin of the regime's wage policy.

With success came a growing confidence and radicalization. In 1979, metalworkers called a general strike for March 13, to demand a pay increase and greater workplace control. The support for the strike call was overwhelming and union assemblies had to be held at the Vila Euclides soccer stadium, the only place capable of holding the 80,000 workers who showed up for the first meeting. Lula described the scene:

> When we [the union directors] arrived, the fences, the stadium, the grass, everything was occupied, and the stage was only a little table. The sound system wasn't sufficient even for a small room. The sound didn't work, and I was alone like a clown on top of the table. Everyone was getting nervous, and the leaders were beginning to disagree right there because the sound system was no good and who knows what else. . . . And the workers said: "Calm down, calm down." You know how we held that assembly? We kept workers there for four hours on the field without sound. . . . I yelled, the people in front repeated it and it was passed backwards. . . . When it started to rain, a few people started to leave, I shouted that no one there would melt [from the rain], and nobody else went away.[15]

Days later, the work stoppage was ruled illegal by a Labor Court. But Lula, showing a growing willingness to confront the authorities (as well as a growing recognition of the need for direct political activity by the working class) told a union assembly, "The strike can be considered illegal, but it is just and legitimate, because its illegality is based on laws that weren't made by us or our representatives." No one returned to work and support for the strikers in the form of food and money, poured in from popular organizations. When police repression and harassment intensified, Bishop Claudio Hummes spoke at a union assembly to offer his backing. "The Church supports the strike because it considers it just and peaceful and hopes that workers will remain united around their leadership," he said.

On March 21, eight days after the strike began, Labor Minister

Murilo Macedo ruled that talks should be held between labor and capital, but insisted on an immediate return to work by the metal-workers – a proposition overwhelmingly rejected by the strikers. Two days later, military police surrounded union headquarters in São Bernardo, Santo Andrade, and São Caetano, and closed them down. Meanwhile the government declared the soccer stadium off-limits to strike assemblies. These moves essentially ended union resistance, and strikers slowly began returning to work. At that point, Lula agreed to a 15 per cent pay rise, far less than strikers had asked for, and promised a forty-five day "truce" with the firms.

Two points were driven home by the strike and its aftermath. First the companies, who promised not to fire any returning strikers and did so anyway, could not be trusted (worse, the layoffs were selective, with union militants targeted to go). Second, given the almost complete lack of support received from congressional representatives, it was clear that workers could not even expect the backing of opposition politicians. Another lesson learned was that strikers should be prepared to confront increased violence from the regime. Whereas in 1978 there were few direct clashes, as most strikers remained on workplace premises, 1979 saw state and capital working hand in hand. Companies forced workers on to the street, and police were soon on hand to repress pickets and other strike activity. "On the street, police can be called upon to resolve disturbances. . . . After 1978, we couldn't use the strategy of strikes inside the companies," Lula later recalled.[16]

This was seen in practice six months after the ABCD stoppages ended, when the São Paulo Metalworkers Union voted to go on strike, and the police acted swiftly and brutally. Churches where support meetings were held were invaded, and, in the worse incident, a soldier shot and killed an important union activist, Santo Dias da Silva, in front of a city factory. The increasing violence did not prevent workers from walking off the job. The year saw a total of 113 strikes, involving some 3.2 million workers in 15 states, which represented one of the biggest strike waves in Brazilian history. The 1979 strikes marked a growing sense of unity among broad categories of the working class, the reemergence of a long-suppressed awareness of class consciousness and collective strength.

As one observer wrote of the period:

In addition to the diversity of positions in the labor market, of conditions

of work and life, of union practice and political barriers, [strikers] identified a common experience of social and political exclusion under the
authoritarian regime. The end of the government's wage policy . . . was
the principal explicit demand of the workers. . . . But there was something
else, a latent demand that made the workers' movement a collective actor
unified in opposition to authoritarianism: the recognition of the dignity of
labor . . . of the [right to] equality in the political arena.[17]

The economy's continued poor performance, and the regime's refusal
to change its wage policy (its only concession was to agree that wages
be readjusted to compensate for inflation every six months, instead of
annually), meant labor disputes were inevitable. On April 1, 1980,
200,000 metalworkers from unions in all four of the ABCD cities
again went on strike, demanding better pay, as well as a reduction of
the forty-eight hour week to forty hours and job stability guarantees.
A labor court first surprised everyone by ruling the strike legal, but
soon reversed the decision under pressure from the military.

The government was increasingly worried about the growing
militancy of the union movement, and tensions ran high. Soon after
the strike began, army helicopters hovered over the Vila Euclides
stadium, again the site of strike meetings, and pointed machineguns at
the assembled multitude of 100,000 workers below. Then, on April
17, the Labor Minister ordered the São Bernardo Metalworkers
Union closed, and stripped Lula of the presidency. Within days, 1,600
union activists, including Lula, had been arrested in an all-out effort to
break the strike. (An older worker, who constructed a barricade of
stones, oildrums and nails at the door of one auto plant, was hauled in
for questioning by the secret police, who accused him of belonging to
the radical underground group "Socialist Convergence." "I've been at
Mercedes Benz for eighteen years and have never worked for that
firm," he replied.[18] Lula and several other top leaders were held in jail
for a month and permanently banned from any sort of labor activities
(an order they subsequently ignored). The soccer stadium was again
closed off to the strikers – meetings were transferred to the patio of the
church in São Bernardo – and the military declared the workers
represented an illegal "pressure group," forbidding companies to
negotiate.

Meanwhile, the strike continued. Union leaders had foreseen swift
state action, and had set up alternative leadership and parallel structures so the stoppage could not be crushed with one swift blow. But

after forty-one days, strikers returned to work without winning their key demands. Nonetheless, the strike represented a growing politicization of the São Paulo working class. Maria Helena Moreira Alves wrote in her book, *State and Opposition in Brazil, 1964-1984*:

> The metalworkers' strike of 1980 made clear the limitations of the "political opening." Popular pressure for participation in governmental decisions would not be tolerated [if it was seen to threaten] the model of economic development. A society defined strictly by the parameters of the Doctrine of National Security and Development is that in which any energetic manifestations of economic and social dissatisfaction constitutes unacceptable "pressure," when [those making the demands] don't belong to the elite. The more organized the initiative, and the more support it has from the population, the more it will be treated as a threat to be eliminated.[19]

As Moreira Alves noted, the military saw the 1980 strike as such a serious threat that it placed the state of São Paulo under the control of the army, with troops occupying most of the cities affected by the strike. After strikers returned to work, the government decreed a new law making strikes in "essential categories" illegal. The term "essential" was broadly defined, and included sectors such as banks, transport, water, gas, electricity, communications, port workers, hospitals, and public services, among others.

The repression against the union movement intensified. In 1981, General Golberry do Couta e Silva, considered the regime's strategic mastermind, said, "Our objective on the labor front is to wipe out a powerful movement that has turned to political provocation. It is a movement led astray by its leaders, who have gone beyond their original field of action."[20]

As part of the strategy, Lula was sentenced that year under the National Security Law to three and a half years in prison. (The verdict was brought to appeal and overturned.)

By this time, the regime was losing control of both the economy (in 1981, GNP fell by 1.9 per cent, with industrial production falling by 7.5 per cent. Meanwhile, inflation soared 97 per cent. After a flat 1982, the next year was one of the country's worst ever: GNP plunged by over 4 per cent while inflation climbed by 239 per cent) as well as the political opening. That fact was reflected in the growing combativeness, and even more so, in the growing prestige, of the "authentics." While traditional leaders, happy to peacefully coexist with the regime's populist labor policies (especially if they continued to control the distribution of handouts), still maintained a good deal of influence, the new unionists were making rapid inroads. At the First National Conference of the Working Class, held in São Paulo state in 1981, the vote was evenly split between the two sides. But a poll conducted among delegates showed 46.5 per cent considered Lula to be the ideal union leader while only 9 per cent pointed to Joaquím dos Santos Andrade, the leading representative of traditional labor.[21]

THE NEW PARTY

The reform law passed in late 1979, which allowed for the creation of new political parties, was central to the dictatorship's policy of controlled "political opening." The military hoped the measure would split the opposition – then concentrated in the MDB – and assumed the labor movement would be safely buried in a new, and reliable, PTB. Things didn't work out exactly as they had planned. First, a popular campaign resulted in the Congress approving earlier that year a broader amnesty than the generals had contemplated. This allowed for the return of scores of political exiles from the exterior, among them Brizola, Prestes, Miguel Arraes (the ex-governor of Pernambuco, who along with Brizola had sent out state troops to oppose the coup), and Fernando Gabeira (an ex-guerrilla who was involved in the kidnapping of the US ambassador in 1970). Their return was celebrated as an end to the military's policy of vetoing the participation in politics of those it deemed to be threats to national security, and increased the pressure for the creation of new parties.[22]

With the December reform, a new party structure emerged. In addition to the new rightist PDS and the heterogeneous (P)MDB, a centrist PTB did begin organizing. But Leonel Brizola, who lost a court bid to recover that party's name, resurrected the spirit of Goulart and Vargas in the new PDT.

Many leftists, suspicious of both the communist parties and Brizola's strand of populism, had long dreamed of forming an independent socialist party. As early as 1977, and during the next two years, a group of São Paulo-based intellectuals and political leaders held periodic meetings with the union "authentics" and discussed the formation of such a party. But insurmountable differences existed, with one group – mostly the former – favoring a focus on congressional activism and a second group – mostly the unionists – wanting to work at the level of popular organizing. As a result, no agreement was reached: the intellectuals and politicians remained tied to the MDB while the labor leaders continued to work for a new party. (There were some important exceptions to the above split. For example, sociologist Francisco Weffort and economist Paul Singer were later to play important roles in the PT.)

When labor conflicts escalated during the late 1970s, the unionists became more convinced than ever that there was a need for a Workers Party. It was no coincidence that the main push came from São Paulo states, specifically in the ABCD region, where almost all the country's most important – and militant – trade unions were located. São Paulo also had a strong core of left-leaning political leaders from the MDB (including five that defected to the PT in 1980, before it was officially recognized, and several others that joined during the next few years) as well as many opposition intellectuals working in universities and research organizations. Finally, within the city there existed a strong network of popular movements, many created with the help of the Church under the leadership of Cardinal Arns. A broad range of groups independent of the Church also existed, or were developing, including black rights organizations, feminist groups and neighborhood associations. Most of these groups were sympathetic to the left, and many, though certainly not all, either backed the PT during its founding or joined later. (The PT was not initially tied to the city's radical left organizations, but a number of clandestine groups, mostly Trotskyite, were involved in the party's founding.)

Lula had wavered over the need for a political party for the working class. In May 1978, he said during a television interview that a party was not necessary: "The situation of the working class, to be resolved, is independent of the creation of a political party. I think the situation of the working class will be resolved when workers participate in political life, independently of the creation or not of a political party." A few months later, he had changed his position, saying the hour had come for the working class to "stop being an instrument. . . . The workers have to create, not just one, but various political parties, that meet all the ideological demands coming from inside the factories."

One reason for the change was the fact that labor could not count on support from opposition politicians. The MDB was already quite strong by 1978, having received a majority of votes cast in that year's federal and state elections, and had its strongest backing in São Paulo and other urban centers. But the party was ideologically mixed, and even most of its "leftist" members only offered tepid support for the working class. (In 1979, when the *ABCD Jornal* monitored Congress, it found that only twelve federal deputies fully backed strikers during the major battles of that year.) Also tending to the conclusion that a political party was necessary was the rapidly emerging consciousness of a linkage between economic and political action. As Lula later said, "It was only with the strikes that we perceived the need for political participation. We saw that the two fields were very tied. That it didn't help to get a 10 per cent pay rise if those who control power have the means to decree a wage policy that takes away all the conquests of the working class."[23]

Lula's support for a new party was still a minority position within the labor movement in late 1978. In December of that year, twelve major leaders (all but one representing unions from São Paulo state) met in São Bernardo do Campo to discuss the question. Only Lula, Skromov, Bittar and Cicotte supported the idea wholeheartedly. As the regime's repression of the union movement increased, though, more and more of the "authentics" switched positions.

Early the next year, the Ninth Congress of Metalworkers, Mechanics and Electricians (representing more than one million workers), meeting in Lins, São Paulo voted in favor of a proposal to create a Workers Party. Though the proposal was rejected by many unionists (including most of Brazil's communists, who predicted the party would not get off the ground), an important faction of the labor movement, including its most dynamic leaders, decided to move forward. On May Day of 1979, the Partido dos Trabalhadores, while still not legally constituted, had activists on the street, distributing a "Statement of Principles." Part of the document said, "In a society such as ours, based on exploitation and inequality among classes, the exploited and oppressed have the permanent necessity to maintain organizations [so that it is] possible to offer resistance . . . to the oppression and privileges of the dominant class. But every time leaders of the workers and oppressed launch the task of constructing such an organization . . . all types of obstacles are placed in their path."[24] The document, which traced the "emancipation" of the working class to the 1978 strike at Saab-Scania, said this time the obstacles would be overcome.

After another nine months of organizing, the PT was officially launched on February 10, 1980, at a meeting attended by 750 people at the Sion School in São Paulo. Of the attendees, 101 signed the founding document (the new party had only about 300 activists at the time), which said, "The PT is born of the will for the political independence of the workers, who are tired of being putty in the hands of politicians and parties committed to the maintenance of the current economic, social and political order . . . [the party] will be the real political expression of all those exploited by the capitalist system." While the political orientation of the party was clearly leftist, Lula made clear at the Sion meeting that defining ideological position would not be the PT's first priority. "It's time to finish with the ideological rustiness and self-indulgence of those who sit at home reading Marx and Lenin. It's time to move from theory to practice. The Workers Party is not the result of any theory but the result of twenty-four hours of practice," he said.

The dominance of labor was seen in the PT's first Provisional Regional Commission, approved in May. Sixty per cent of its members were tied to unions: the other 40 per cent were mostly politicians, journalists and representatives from extreme left groups. In a sharp break with past Brazilian practice, the PT created a structure that allowed for real grassroots control of the party, with all members tied to a small *nucleo de base* (core group), at which level all important decisions would be taken. Once decisions were made, members were expected to abide by them. The system created a mix between total grassroots control and the Leninist conception of the vanguard.[25]

While union and other organizing continued, the PT still had to obtain recognition from the country's Electoral Court in order to run in the 1982 elections. By the end of 1981, it had completed the registration process by establishing directories in one-fifth of all counties in nineteen different states, and had a combined membership of about half a million militants.[26] The PT gained its first elected officials before even competing in an election: five federal deputies, eight state deputies, twenty-seven members of City Councils, and one mayor, all joined as the party was being formed.

The government and the right did everything possible to prevent the party's growth. In mid-1980, General Golbery told a conference at the Superior War School that Lula's end was at hand, "as a union leader, which he will stop being, and as a political leader, which he will not become."[27] He failed to explain how that end would be brought about, but incidents took place that suggested he was not talking about defeat at the polls. Earlier that year, the party's offices in Campo

Grande (in the south-central state of Mato Grosso do Sul) were burned to the ground; activists in several other regions were arrested for promoting the new party. In February 1981, fifteen party members were arrested in the states of Amazonas, Ceara, Bahia, Brasília, and São Paulo, for protesting against the scheduled trial of Lula and twelve other union leaders. A month later, the PT's headquarters in São Paulo were burgled. Documents and other materials were taken, and though no proof was even found, party leaders suspected it was the work of the military. By that time, over thirty party members, Lula among them, were facing prosecution under the National Security Law.

Despite such harassment, the PT established itself as the first political party in the country's history that was not formed at the behest of the elite. While many ideological positions were still to be worked out, party leaders were unanimous in their support for socialism. Lula said that Brazilian capitalism was not capable of meeting the needs of the poor, "because of the economic ties that the county has, of the almost absolute dependence of our economy on the developed countries . . . [not just] the foreign debt, but also the problem of priorities, of models." He also rejected social democracy, saying it could "only exist to the extent that there are slaves in Latin America, Central America, Asia and Africa."[28]

Lula believed it was crucial that the PT develop a Brazilian model of socialism and not emulate the experience of other countries. During a 1982 interview he said, " Does Cuban socialism interest us? Russian? Polish? That no longer interests the Poles. . . . The role of the PT is not to get a blueprint of the Chinese revolution and do the same thing in Brazil. We want to know; in terms of our reality, what is it that we can do?"[29] A keen sensitivity to that question would serve the party well during the following years, as the PT expanded beyond its foothold in São Paulo and the industrialized southeast, and gained ground in the country's vast interior.[30]

NOTES

1. In the late 1970s, the then US President Jimmy Carter outraged the generals by inviting Arns to ride to the airport with him in the presidential limousine at the end of a visit to the country. While most First World leftists criticized Carter's human rights policy as pure public relations, an attempt to score points on the Soviet Union in the international arena – an argument not without merit – many Brazilians say there was a

real impact locally. Liberation theologist Leonardo Boff said torture "stopped" due to Carter's declarations. In a 1988 interview with one of the authors, shortly before the US presidential election between George Bush and Michael Dukakis, he expressed dismay upon hearing that some US leftists would not vote as they considered the two candidates almost equally bad. "That may be true for the United States, but it's not for the Third World," he said.

2. March 2, 1987.

3. Maria Herminia Tavares de Almeida, "O sindicalismo brasileiro entre a conservação e a mudança," in *Sociedade e politica no brasil pos-64*, pp. 199-200.

4. Ibid., p. 210. Most union officials managed quite well under the paternalistic labor code, particularly since they received funds from the government, collected from workers' pay. "While leftist unions financed strikes, we bought and constructed buildings," Antonio Alves de Almeida, longstanding president of the National Confederation of Commerce Workers (CNTC) candidly confessed to a newspaper reporter in September 1990. The Confederation's headquarters in Brasília proudly boasted a bronze plaque outside saying the huge structure of 6,500 square meters, surrounded by an artificial lake, had been constructed entirely with funds taken out of workers' pay. "When we tell people this is a house of the workers, nobody believes it," Alves said. Another conservative group, the National Confederation of Workers in Industry, used its money to build a "Technical Center of Union Education," replete with an indoor soccer arena, basketball courts, and an Olympic-sized pool. *Jornal do Brasil*, September 9, 1990.

5. Rachel Meneguello, *PT-A Formação de Um Partido 1979-1982*, p. 43.

6. In a 1978 essay, "The World Cup and Its Pomp," Umberto Eco sarcastically deplores soccer fanaticism: "I approve of it and consider it providential. Those crowds of fans, cut down by heart attacks in the grandstands, those referees who pay for a Sunday's fame by personal exposure to grievous bodily harm . . . those celebrating young men who speed drunkenly through the street in the evening . . . those families financially destroyed after succumbing to insane scalpers. . . . They fill my heart with joy. I am in favor of soccer passion as I am in favor of drag-racing, of competition between motorcycles on the edge of a cliff, and of wild parachute jumping, mystical mountain climbing, crossing oceans in rubber dinghies, Russian roulette, and the use of narcotics."

Eco thus shows why intellectuals so often have no idea of what takes place in the real world. While it may be true that modern-day sports is nothing more than distraction for the masses and the commercialization of leisure, it is impossible to understand a nation without some comprehension of what drives its people – such as Brazilians and their soccer madness. The generals who ran the country were greatly helped by the nationwide celebration that followed the country's triumph in the 1970 World Cup – some people say they had four years of peace, until the national team was eliminated from the tournament in 1974. And in 1990, some economists were reportedly making dual projections for the year: one based on Brazil winning that year's World Cup in Rome, and the other if it didn't.

7. Frei Betto, *Lula, Biografia Politica de Um Operario*, p. 17; Maria Helena Moreira Alves, *O Estado e Oposição no Brasil*, p. 248.

8. *Lula, Sem Censura*, p. 19.

9. Marcio Morel, *Lula, O Metalurgico, Anatomia de uma Liderança*, p. 107.

10. *Lula, Sem Censura*, p. 29.

11. Morel, p.108.

12. The metalworkers were paid miserably during the period, but received more than almost any other category of worker. Statistics compiled by a labor group showed that average 1978 pay for workers in the Brazilian automobile industry was the

equivalent of 60 cents per hour! Comparative figures in other national auto industries at the time were $8.65 in the United States, $5.65 in West Germany, and $3.45 in England. In the survey, workers from just two countries had lower salaries than in Brazil: Argentine ($0.55) and the Philippines ($0.35). While Brazil's autoworkers, underpaid as they were, amounted to the country's "labor aristocracy," the strikes at the end of the decade showed they did not act like one.

13. Morel, p. 112.

14. *The New York Times,* June 22, 1978.

15. *Lula, Sem Censura,* p. 54.

16. Alves, p. 253.

17. Maria Herminia Tavares de Almeida, "O sindicalismo brasileiro entre a conservação e a mudanca," in *Sociedade e politica no brasil pos-64,* p. 207.

18. Morel, p. 128.

19. Alves, p. 261.

20. *The New York Times,* March 3, 1981.

21. *Isto É,* September 2, 1981.

22. The military accepted the amnesty because it also stipulated that no one would be prosecuted for political crimes committed during the dictatorship. While the Brazilian regime did not engage in wholesale slaughter, as did their counterparts in Chile and Argentina, they systematically violated human rights. Official estimates are that 200 of the government's "enemies" were killed, several hundred "disappeared" and thousands were tortured. As a result of the amnesty, hundreds of those directly involved in torture, murder and other human rights violations retained their positions in the police and armed forces after the return of civilian rule.

23. *ABCD Jornal,* December, 1979.

24. Moacir Gadotti and Otaviano Pereira, *Pra Que PT?,* pp. 33-4.

25. Michael Löwy, "A New Type of Party, The Brazilian PT," *Latin American Perspectives,* Fall 1987, p. 457.

26. Alves, p. 276.

27. Cited in *Isto É,* August 25, 1982.

28. Ibid.

29. *Lula, Sem Censura,* p. 84.

30. The PT did sometimes lose itself in crude ideological discussions which had little to do with Brazilian reality. Frei Betto, the Dominican friar and political activist who has long been a close colleague of Lula's, and of many other union leaders, has written of the problem:

"Social reality, in contrast to political theory, does not allow for the concealment of facts . . . our reality presents a profile that the alchemy of the left does not always take into account, losing itself in Byzantine discussions that [are] nothing more than a mechanical transposition of beliefs adequate to European or Asian reality to the ground we walk on. . . . No matter how much the positivist biases of some sectors of the PT try to ignore the force of tradition and religious sentiment in the ideology of the Brazilian people, the question will inevitably have to be faced head on, especially as countless militants and leaders of the party had their political origins in Church movements." Frei Betto, p. 63.

4

Agrarian Reform and the PT's Growth in the Interior

The PT intends to be, pure and simply, the expression of the popular movements.

> Lula, when the party was founded

We are the people of the nation. We are the people of God. We want land on earth. We already have it in heaven.

> Pedro Casaldáliga, bishop, activist, and poet

During the early 1980s, the PT was still largely a regional party whose popular appeal and membership were concentrated overwhelmingly in the southeast, and especially São Paulo. At the end of 1982, the party had 245,000 members, with 64,000 concentrated in São Paulo, 35,000 in Minas Gerais, 36,000 in Rio de Janeiro, and 16,000 in Rio Grande do Sul.[1] But the party slowly began to organize in other regions, most importantly the poor interior in the north and northeast. Much of the growth can be attributed to the work of progressive Catholic activists, and the PT's commitment to agrarian reform (which Church militants strongly backed).

As stated earlier, while the Church had initially supported the coup, it had moved into the opposition by the late 1960s.[2] And for much of the dictatorship period, just about the only sort of popular organizing allowed by the regime took place under the umbrella of the Church, which has tremendous moral authority in Brazil – some 85 per cent of the population profess to be Catholic (even though their version of Catholicism may be mixed with aspects of Macumba and Candomblé, which have African and Indian roots).

What Church officials, from bishops down to grassroots activists, experienced and witnessed in the vast interior converted more than a few to progressive activism – specifically, the tremendously unjust distribution of land and the military government's failure to do anything about it. The structure of landowning had been a perennial question in Brazil ever since the Portuguese divided the country during the period of colonization into fourteen *capitaneas*, each controlled by a powerful ally of the King. The call for reform became extremely loud in the early 1960s after "peasant leagues" in the northeast organized and spread quickly. In March 1964, President Goulart promised a massive crowd at a political rally in Rio de Janeiro that he would begin an agrarian reform program by appropriating public lands. Just two weeks later, the coup toppled him from power, and his views on the land question were certainly a key factor in the armed forces' decision to act.

The military regime vowed to give land to millions of peasant families, but like most of their promises of social reform, it never went very far. Among the most impoverished areas was the huge Amazon region (the so-called "Legal Amazon," a geographical division created by the military, covering nine states and 2 million square miles), where the generals' policies of promoting export agriculture – partly via subsidies for wealthy farmers who cleared and, in theory, developed land – heightened land concentration and resulted in violent conflicts between long-time squatters and rich newcomers. The latter included many southern industrialists, bankers and multinational corporations, all whom were enticed by the military's generous benefits. If peasants already claimed the land, the newcomers often cheated them out of it – or simply employed gunmen to scare them away, or worse.

The generals also implemented or promoted a number of "Great Projects" – huge, multibillion-dollar development projects that often relied upon large inputs of overseas capital. One example was the Carajás agricultural and mining project, dreamed up in the late 1960s. The project, located in the southeastern Amazon in Para state, covers an area of 345,000 square miles – the size of France, Italy and Holland combined – and sits atop huge reserves of iron, nickel, tin, aluminium and other ores and minerals. It received funding from the World Bank and other international lenders, and has produced vast deforestation. Also, the project occupies territory that had been claimed by Indian tribes as well as poor peasants.

The Church became increasingly allied with the peasantry as conflicts heated up. In 1976, one year after creating Pastoral Land Commission (CPT) to advise and assist peasant families, the National Conference of Brazilian Bishops (CNBB) released a document sharply critical of the generals, which read, in part:

> The ideology of national security, placed above personal security, is spreading over Latin America, as occurred in countries under Soviet dominion. Inspired by it, regimes of force refer to the war they are waging against communism and in favor of economic development, and brand as subversive all those who do not agree with their authoritarian view of the organization of society. The training for this war against subversion leads to an increase in the brutality employed by its agents and creates a new type of fanaticism and a climate of violence and fear.[3]

During the following years, Church leaders heightened their criticism of the regime and, crucially, moved from merely attacking the government to calling for greater public participation in organizing and running the country's affairs. Religious officials were especially outspoken on the question of agrarian reform. In 1978, the CNBB published a paper on the issue which said:

> The injustices in the occupation and use of the land have grown worse as a result of pressure exercised . . . on those who live on and from the land. . . . The big official projects turn small landowners and peasant farmers off the land, pay them unjust prices after long delays, [and] also force unprepared and penniless peasants to live as social outcasts on the edge of the cities. The abiding injustice has been maintained by institutionalized violence, by repressive forces operating outside the law and enjoying the omission, complacency or connivance of the authorities and thus, provoking desperate reactions which provide a pretext for even more violent repression.[4]

One of the most important concrete contributions of Church activists was the establishment of numerous "Ecclesiastical Base Communities" in rural areas. The Communities, which generally have an average of about forty members, are often run by lay people. All include bible studies among their activities, but most devote much of the time to organizing community development projects, such as schools, health posts, and agricultural improvements.

The Communities began to organize in Brazil in the early 1960s. Initially, their advocates saw them not as political vehicles, but more as a means for the Church to spread the gospel through the vast interior, especially as there were not enough priests available to pay regular visits to all villages. (One of their early proponents was Eugenio Sales, now the archbishop of Rio, and a prominent member of the conservative wing.) The Communities really took off, though, after the 1968 meeting of Latin American bishops at Medellín Colombia, which called upon the Church to exercise a "preferential option for the poor." They spread especially quickly during the dictatorship, as labor union and political party activities were severely restricted, and they also began to play a more clearly social role. By the 1980s, an estimated 100,000 Base Communities existed in Brazil, and most have a progressive political orientation.[5]

Many Church officials offered more active support to the rural poor as well. One of the most outspoken defenders of the peasantry was Bishop Pedro Casaldáliga, a Spaniard who came to Mato Grosso state in central Brazil in 1968. Casaldáliga covered much of his huge 150,000 square-kilometer diocese (almost the size of Portugal) by bus and on foot, and his support for landless peasants was largely responsible for the seven threats of expulsion he received from the generals, and the innumerable death threats he received from the region's landowners.

He also aroused the ire of TV Globo. In 1977, Edgardo Erichsen, then director of the network, bitterly attacked Casaldáliga on a nationally televised program, saying, "It seems that the bishop has exchanged his crucifix and rosary for the hammer and sickle, his prayer book for the thoughts of Mao Tse-tung, his priestly piety for violence and that he is only waiting for the right moment to exchange his cassock for a guerrilla's uniform. Of some left-wing priests it can be said that they light one candle to God and the other to the devil. But for Bishop Dom Pedro Maria Casaldáliga, the least that can be said is that he lights both candles to the devil."[6] The Spaniard's crime was to have encouraged peasants to form unions, and otherwise stand up for their legal rights, which entitled them to work their land. And Casaldáliga was just one – though certainly among the most radical – of hundreds of bishops and priests who actively campaigned on behalf of the peasantry.[7]

The landless also gained an important ally with the birth of the PT in 1980. While some other parties voiced support for land reform – and some elected officials from these parties, in fact, died as a result of their efforts – the PT was the first to make land reform one of its top priorities. Activists and leaders, including Lula, visited rural areas in the early 1980s to assist peasants, offer advice on organizing, publicize violence against rural workers, and, of course, to encourage and set up PT chapters. In many cases, the first people to adhere to the new party were local Church and peasant activists who were already involved in the struggle to form unions and defend squatters (in numerous cases there was – and is – almost no difference between membership lists at the union, the Base Community, and the PT). And as the PT's commitment to the issue became clear – through its calls for land reform at the national level and its continuing support at the local level – the party gained many adherents (an added boost, to both peasants and the PT's growth in the interior, came with the founding of the CUT. Many rural unions soon joined the federation, and CUT led aggressive organizing drives throughout the interior).

But despite the Church's support for the landless, and the added aid offered by the PT and the CUT, the peasantry's situation deteriorated through the final years of military rule. Between 1979 and 1985, almost 800 people were killed in land conflicts, with 222 being murdered in the latter year alone (most of those killed during 1985 died after the civilian government took charge in March). Brazil emerged from the dictatorship with one of the most regressive patterns of landholding in the world. Around 5 per cent of the population owned 95 per cent of the arable land. In addition, only about one-fifth of the potentially productive land was regularly worked. The rest lay idle, while Brazil spent billions of dollars importing foodstuffs.

For the new civilian government, a major problem in addressing the situation was the pattern of landholding established under military rule. While the traditional landholders remained powerful, foreign multinationals and domestic industrialists and bankers acquired huge tracts of land when the generals were in office. Thus, any program of agricultural reform would necessarily have to affect all sectors of the ruling elite.

Sarney, in his first proposal, promised to expropriate all the holding of the latifundias (the huge, unproductive estates that dominate the countryside), and to resettle 15 million peasant families over a fifteen-year period. But after encountering fierce opposition from landowners (and from the extremely influential SNI, Brazil's then national intelligence agency) the plan was rewritten twelve times over a six month period. In the final document, released in October 1985, the reform plan was drastically curtailed, calling for the redistribution of 43 million hectares and the resettlement of 1.4 million families over four years. That would have affected only 10 per cent of the 430 million hectares of latifundia lands, and assisted less than 12 per cent of Brazil's estimated 12 million landless peasants. Despite being dissatisfied with the changes, the left hoped that at least those targets would be met. Both sides in the conflict geared up for battle.

The two major organizations of the landless were (and are) the National Confederation of Agricultural Workers (CONTAG) and the movement of Rural Workers Without Land (MST). CONTAG is far larger and better organized, but the MST has grown in strength and is considered more radical, and a bigger threat, by the landowners. Both of these groups, and especially the latter, have strong connections with the PT and CUT.

CONTAG is a national confederation which brings together federations and local unions. The organization was founded in 1963, but with the coup a year later the military government stripped it of its leaders and temporarily shut it down. During the dictatorship, the Confederation grew rapidly, but, as was the case in the rest of the labor movement, the activities of its affiliates were strictly controlled and it was not known for its militancy. Even so, CONTAG emerged from the period of military rule with almost 3,000 member unions and nearly 10 million members, and agrarian reform was its main banner.

The MST was founded in 1984 by peasants who had participated in land takeovers in the southern part of the country. One of the group's leaders, Walcyr Guzzoni, once explained that land occupations simply "signify the retaking of land that is already ours . . . because God made the land for all men and not only for a few." In 1986, the MST coordinated some fifty land occupations, involving about 100,000 peasants.

The Church, whilst not officially backing the MST's promotion of land invasions, said they resulted from the desperation of the poor. In 1986, José Gomes, then head of the CPT, said it was "important to distinguish between what is legal and what is legitimate. . . . The right to a dignified life is superior to any law."

The right organized as well. The most reactionary of the land-owners rallied behind Ronaldo Caiado, an ultraconservative rancher who helped form the Rural Democratic Union (UDR) in 1985. The group, which claimed to have close ties to military officials, claimed it supported Sarney's plan, but that Church and government land should be expropriated before private property was touched. Meanwhile, the UDR organized to make sure the land reform program never got off the ground.

The UDR viciously attacked peasant groups, and claimed they were carrying out subversive activities. The organization's vice-president, Salvador Farina, accused the MST of carrying out, "disgraceful work, taking advantage of the humble classes . . . and inducing violence. Their philosophy of hatred and class struggle contributes nothing to the security of Brazil." UDR representatives also liked to claim landless peasants were being funded and guided by the hidden hand of Moscow or Peking, though a majority of the rural poor would certainly not be able to locate either the Soviet Union or China on a map.

One of the UDR's earliest activities was an auction of several thousand head of cattle, supposedly to raise funds to support candidates in the 1986 congressional elections. Later, a prominent official from the group admitted the money garnered was used to buy arms.[8]

Besides the UDR, other producer groups worked to defeat the agrarian reform. Especially important were the national Confederation of Agricultural Producers and the rightist Brazilian Rural Society (many considered the UDR to be an armed extension of the latter). Political lobbying by these groups fell on sympathetic ears, as a majority of congressmen were landowners (as were Sarney and then Justice Minister Paulo Brossard).

As is usual in Brazil, the powerful won the battle. The government never came close to meeting even its reduced targets for land reform. In 1986, the plan's first full year, only about 22 per cent of the land targeted for expropriation actually changed hands. An even smaller percentage of families that were to be settled actually received title to property. An estimate that year by the Rio-based National Campaign for Agrarian Reform projected that if the first-year pace continued, Brazil's landless families would finally be settled in the year 3042.[9]

The program continued to crawl along at a snail's pace in the following years, and the potential for significant land reform was formally gutted when the Constituent Assembly included a clause in the 1988 constitution that protected "productive" land from expropriations. (The vote was 267 for, 253 against, and 11 abstentions. PT Federal Deputy Plínio Sampaio, one of the party's specialists on agrarian reform, called it the "Constituent Assembly's darkest day.") Large landowners have long avoided having their properties seized by putting a few head of cattle out to graze, as a show of usage. The constitution did include provision that required landowners to protect the environment and obey labor laws. But rules such as these are almost completely ignored in Brazil, especially in the countryside, where the rich are almost completely immune from any sort of "justice." (They normally either exercise it or buy it. In rural areas, local county and even state employees, such as schoolteachers, are rarely paid the legal minimum wage – the possibility of peasants having their rights respected is about zero.) The PT and other leftist parties wanted non-compliance with the law to be criteria for expropriation, but this plank was also defeated.

A look at one important region of conflict in the land reform question may help better explain the issue, and the PT's growth in the interior.

THE PARROT'S BEAK

The Parrot's Beak region in the southeastern Amazon (so named because of its shape), located in Tocantins state (formerly northern Goiás) at its junction with Maranhão and Pará, has long been at the heart of the land conflict. Other than the level of violence there, which is far above average, the battles that have been waged are typical of those fought throughout much of the country's interior. (Even during the period of military rule, the area was notorious for the brutality employed by landowners against the peasantry. Violence was so intense that the armed forces were compelled to create a special "Executive Group" to mediate disputes.)

The Parrot's Beak is an area of incredible natural beauty, being bounded on the west by the Tocantins river and on the east by the Araguaiana, two of the country's most exquisite waterways. It is also a region of extreme poverty, where most peasants live in mud huts covered with palm leaves, and where the dirt roads that run through the area are virtually impassable during the six-month rainy season between November and May.

The military's promotion of export-oriented agriculture had been especially pronounced in the Amazon, including the Parrot's Beak. Hundreds of investors took the generals' bait of public subsidies, with the majority setting up cattle ranches – often with very few cattle on huge tracts of land – in order to receive funding. Billions of dollars in public money were doled out between 1965 and 1983. And 10,000 miles of new roads were built in the late 1960s and early 1970s, greatly increasing access to the region and creating a huge rise in land values – which led to many investors buying land in the Amazon as a speculative hedge against growing inflation.

Conflicts quickly arose, as sections of the region had been occupied by poor subsistence farmers who had moved to the Amazon as a result of land shortages and perennial drought in the northeast. In the Parrot's Beak, many of the peasants had moved to the area as early as the 1940s and 1950s. According to Brazilian land law, peasants who occupy and cultivate their property for more than a year acquire certain rights – becoming *posseiros* – which prevent their expulsion without a legal hearing. Those who work the same land for more than ten years have legal rights to the property. The law in Brazil, though, is rarely enforced when it comes to protecting the rights of the poor, and many peasants were illegally evicted.

For the many that had lost their property, or who came to the Parrot's Beak after the military policies had resulted in a flood of wealthy farmers buying, or stealing, most of the land, the only means of survival was working on one of the cattle ranches that cover most of the area – often for as little as $10 a month. Until recently, that was the condition of almost all the peasants who lived there. During the past ten years, though, hundreds of peasant families have won title to their land, despite an organized, brutal campaign of violence waged against them by local landowners. If asked, almost every poor farmer in the region who has managed to secure title to the land will say the reason they managed to hold on was the assistance of the CPT activists, especially a Roman Catholic priest named Josimo.

Josimo Moraes Tavares, a 33-year-old black priest, arrived in the Parrot's Beak in the early 1980s. He was murdered in May 1985, when serving as the regional coordinator of the Pastoral Land Commission. That alone was enough to earn him the hatred of the Parrot's Beak's large landowners. But what marked Josimo to die was his special stature with the *posseiros*. Black and poor, like many of the region's peasants, he was able to understand their needs, hope and pain. Friar Henriqué des Rossiers, a French Dominican who continues to work in the Parrot's Beak and knew Josimo well, said the priest "had a special charisma, a means of communicating with the poor, which was something different from what the rest of us [CPT activists] possessed."[10]

Until Josimo's arrival in the region, religion was a force largely allied with the landowners. Most local priests expressed little interest in the plight of the poor. "Before Josimo arrived, our priest said the poor suffered because that's what God wanted, that we had to put our trust in God," said Francisca Perreira Viera, a peasant activist. "But God doesn't want the poor to be thrown off their lands, and God alone won't solve our problems – our struggle will. We learned that from the Bible, from the courses Josimo taught us."

Josimo worked throughout the region, and his primary text was the Bible. Thanks largely to his work, Base Communities sprang up throughout the Parrot's Beak. One story the priest taught was of the Jews of the Old Testament, a people, he said, who had been dispossessed and persecuted but came together and emerged victorious. (This may sound reactionary to some, if looked at from the perspective of the twentieth-century conflict in the Middle East, but the Israeli–Palestinian conflict is not familiar to many Brazilian peasants.) His vision struck a resonant chord and mobilized the region's peasants in a way that political appeals alone could not. Of course, peasants who are fighting against the government and local landowners to gain title to their land, and form labor unions, quickly gain a political consciousness.

Josimo did not become a member of the PT after the party began organizing in the region (in 1982) but he was a strong sympathizer And while he did not promote the PT, there was such an undeniable link between the party's proposals and the ideas of Church activists that an informal alliance between the two existed. Adilar Daltoe, a CPT leader who replaced Josimo as head of the organization in the region when the latter was murdered, explained the relationship between the party and the Church group:

> The CPT is non-partisan and we are totally independent of the PT. But there was a very natural alliance between our activities, due to an almost complete overlapping of views on the question of agrarian reform. And the movement towards the PT was also strong among many peasants, which we had nothing to do with. The same people who participated in the land struggle and the union movement were drawn to the new party for obvious reasons. Many understand that the PT represented the only possibility for institutional change.

Daltoe also said that the new party was the first to have ever expressed support for the rural poor. "We had never received any real help from political parties or elected officials prior to the PT's birth – we were alone. The parties that existed in the region were so clearly representative of the *latifundiários* it never even occurred to us that we could have their backing. The PT was the first party that had a different proposal, not only in a political (ideological) sense but also in concrete support for the peasants. Later, some politicians from other parties offered help, but the PT broke the ice." He said the PT's help was especially important in denouncing violence against rural workers at the national level, and trying to get the press to report on the situation.[11]

On May 10, 1985, Josimo left his mother, Olinda, at the parish house in São Sebastião do Tocantins. He headed for the CPT's regional office in the city of Imperatriz, some 150 kilometers to the east. Just a few weeks earlier, Josimo had escaped an assassination attempt, when a passing car shot six bullets into the blue Toyota jeep he used to travel through the area.

Olinda, a thin, frail woman of forty-nine, had married at the age of fourteen and been widowed two years later. Her only other child, a daughter, died after a cold turned to pneumonia and there was no money to pay for a doctor. After the first attempt on her son's life, Dona Olinda had become extremely nervous, but Josimo assured her he would be back the next day – Mother's Day, in fact.

He arrived in Imperatriz around midday and parked the jeep. As he climbed the stairs to the CPT office, Geraldo Rodrigues, a gunman hired by local landowners and paid a few hundred dollars, called out his name. When Josimo turned, he fired. The first shot missed. The second, fired as the priest ran up the stairs, hit him in the back. Three hours later Josimo was dead.[12]

Over 3,000 people, mostly peasants but including a contingent of 120 bishops and priests, attended the priest's funeral. Casaldáliga told the then Minister of Agrarian Reform, Nelson Ribeiro (who had strong Church support), "You, who are an honorable man, should resign your office immediately, to preserve your dignity."[13] It was advice he soon heeded.

The landowners who hired Josimo's killer imagined that his death would demoralize the peasants and end their resistance. The night he was murdered, members of the UDR toasted his death with champagne in the area's finest hotel. Francisco Barbosa Dias, a peasant leader in the region said, "Josimo was the most important piece in our struggle. Those men that took our priest must have said, 'Taking this black man is going to demoralize them. They'll end this silly struggle for land.' But they were wrong. They took Padre Josimo but our organization and resistance grew.''

Raimunda Gomes da Silva, a peasant union leader known throughout the Parrot's Beak, explained why: "He gave his life for us. To abandon the work he had done would have meant his blood was lost for nothing.''

The CPT, founded at the national level in 1975, became firmly established in the Parrot's Beak three years later when the area was already considered a hotspot in the land war. Nicola Arponi, a remarkable Italian missionary, set off alone, on foot, visiting villages in the region. He told *posseiros* they had the right to the land, and encouraged the formation of unions to defend those rights. A year later, he was kidnapped by soldiers and beaten and tortured for three days before being released.

Friar des Rossiers arrived in the Parrot's Beak precisely at this time, and he and Nicola continued to work in the region. For the next year, they travelled alone, counseling peasants and denouncing violence against them to the press, the government, international groups, and anyone else who would listen. According to des Rossiers, the Parrot's Beak at the time was "an incredible place, ridden with almost unimaginable poverty. Most peasants had been driven away, and those that remained paid rents of up to 50 per cent of their crops to work land that had once been their own. There were *grilheiros* [land thieves] everywhere, *pistoleiros* everywhere. The peasants were terrorized. People thought they had no rights, that it was a normal situation, that life was meant to be like that.''

The CPT strengthened its presence in the region over the next few years. Josimo, who was named the parish priest in the village of São Sebastião do Tocantins in 1982, began working with the agency, the same year. But while the Commission's arrival was the catalyst for change in the Parrot's Beak, there would have been no victories if not for a group of remarkable and courageous peasants. Year after year, landowners, judges, and police officials demanded they abandon their land. Year after year they refused to do so. When they were violently expelled from their lands, many returned to rebuild. Not coincidentally, almost all those who won their rights developed a very high level of political *conscientizacão*, and belonged to Base Communities, unions, and the PT.

Miguel Elousa Rojo, a Spanish priest who replaced Josimo in São Sebastião do Tocantins, said: "The Parrot's Beak became famous not because of violence but because of the resistance to that violence." The former, he points out, is common in Brazil. The latter is not.

The story of Maria Senhora Carvalho da Silva is similar to that of many peasants in the region. A black woman of forty-one, she came to the Parrot's Beak from the neighboring state of Maranhão in 1968 with her husband, Vale, whom she married when she was twelve years old, and the couple's two young children (the family has since grown to include four more offspring). Despite the fact that the couple has been happily married, she has never forgiven the priest who performed the ceremony.

The family's first stop was a village called Vila União, where twenty families had arrived years earlier, including that of Maria's brother. "He sent a letter saying it was good there, that there was a lot of land. Soon after, my mother went there and shortly after I joined them," she remembered.

Accompanying Maria were Vale and the couple's two children, and they discovered that her brother's claims were true. "It was pure virgin forest. The land didn't have an owner and we didn't want to be its owner. We just wanted to work," she said. They did exactly that for seven years, until the police arrived and upheld a landowner's claim to the area. Vale signed away his rights – without knowing he had any – in front of the police and vice-mayor of the municipality, as did the other families. "We didn't know anything. We thought, 'We've been without land so often, we can be again,'" Maria said.

A number of the families stayed together, and founded a new community thirty-five kilometers from Vila União, near the edge of the Tocantins river. In the Parrot's Beak, though, each passing year saw a growing share of the land claimed by the new arrivals from the south, and peasants were expelled more and more quickly as time passed. Maria remembered that sixty troopers from the military police showed up in the village early one morning two years after they had arrived. "They came with landowners and *pistoleiros*, burned down all the homes, and told us not to come back," she said.

In some ways, Maria is lucky. After moving once again, she and her family won title to a piece of land in a village called Centro dos Mulatos. A nearby neighbor is Domingos Gomes da Costa. Married,

with two small boys, he worked for about 90 cents a day, clearing land
on a ranch ten kilometers from his hut. He arrived in the region in
1983, after being evicted from land on three occasions. Seven years
before coming to the village, he was living with his parents in a tiny
village along with five other families. "One day, a landowner came
with a government official," he recalled. "The official said he needed
to pay the landowner 500 cruzeiros to stay – that was a lot of money
then. My father arranged the money, but he told the man he'd only
pay it to someone from the government, not directly to him."

Soon after, Domingos was working on the family's plot of land,
planting rice, alongside both his parents. Two *pistoleiros* sent by the
landowner showed up and savagely beat his mother. When his father
went to defend her, they stabbed him through the stomach with a
machete. He and his mother also suffered knife wounds. Two days
later, his father, Sandoval, died; his mother spent two months in the
hospital recovering. The other five families in the village were terrorized and fled the region.

Stories like Domingos's are not uncommon in the Parrot's Beak,
and violence escalated when Sarney came to power promising agrarian reform. Nowhere was the situation worse than the Parrot's Beak.
In late 1985, in an incident that was similar to countless others
occurring in the region, 160 members of the military police and a
group of *pistoleiros* burned the homes and crops of peasants in a small
village called São Pedro. Most had lived there for thirty years. "They
spent four days in the village, looking for the men," remembered
trade union representative José Alves de Souza, "but we'd fled to the
forest. When we returned, *pistoleiros* were still in the area, and we
never knew if they'd act again."

A month later, after remaining in the village and trying to rebuild,
José and two friends, Raimundo da Souza and Luís Mendes de
Carvalho, were walking to their plots of land at around 6 a.m. Luís
was in front, when suddenly three *pistoleiros* opened fire. "Luís was
shot above the left breast and dropped immediately. Raimundo and I
were wounded, but escaped and hid in the woods," Jośe said.

Several days later, Luís died, and his death had a chilling impact on
São Pedro. No one worked the land, except in large groups organized
by the local union, with help coming from peasants in nearby communities. According to José, "After he was shot, it was as if no one lived
in the village. Even the dogs didn't bark." And Raimundo said: "São

Pedro was deathly quiet. If a child started to cry, his mother covered his mouth and said, 'Son, don't cry, there are gunmen out there.' "

No official investigation was ever launched into Luís's death, though witnesses from the village saw the gunmen disappear on to a landowner's estate. Nor did peasants expect that one would be, as the local police chief was the ex-manager of the estate where the *pistoleiros* vanished.

Luís was just one of about 800 people murdered in land conflicts during the five-year "New Republic" (far more, in fact, than any comparable period of the dictatorship). Almost 150 were killed in the Parrot's Beak and surrounding areas alone during 1985 and 1986. But in only two of all of the cases – that of Josimo's killer and in the case of two brothers who murdered an Italian priest – were the gunmen sentenced to prison. In not a single case were the landowners who hired the killers brought to justice.

Despite Brazil's traditional machismo, which is especially strong in rural areas, more and more of the Parrot's Beak political leaders are women. One of the most important is Raimunda Gomes da Silva, who was a close friend of Josimo's. (Her husband, Antonio, himself a prominent activist, backed her involvement in political organizing, but believed the concept "Men above all," is confirmed in the Bible. "When he tells me that, I tell him that part of the Bible was written by a 'machista'," Raimunda said.) She came to northeastern Tocantins (then Goiás) state in 1980, and settled in the small village of Sete Barracas, which sits between two large cattle ranches. She studied the Bible with Josimo after he arrived in the region, and it is the Bible, she says, that "gives the force of faith." For Raimunda, God does not want some to eat while others go hungry, and clearly sides with the poor. "The rich man who prays in church and pays a *pistoleiro* to kill a worker doesn't have a kingdom waiting in heaven," she said.

The CUT-affiliated Rural Workers Union of Itaguatins (the municipality in which Sete Barracas is located) was founded in 1983, after Raimunda and other key activists visited almost every village in the area – on foot – to enlist supporters. The primary purpose of every union in the Parrot's Beak – and most of the region is now unionized after years of organizing – is to secure land for its members. When Raimunda arrived, Sete Barracas had approximately 150 families. By 1985, that figure had fallen to 52, as a neighboring landowner had bought out or scared off the rest. And that September, 160 members of the military police arrived and kicked everyone off the land, burning most of their homes and crops as well. The man who claimed he had title to the area then placed fifteen *pistoleiros* on the property in order to prevent anyone from returning. For months, the peasants stayed with friends and families in nearby villages. The CPT filed a suit against the new "landowner," protesting against their expulsion, and the union and local PT chapter organized support – material and moral – throughout the region.

And then, said Raimunda, "We had a little help from God." What happened next is now referred to by all who currently live in Sete Barracas as "The Miracle of Roque Santeiro". "Roque Santeiro" was a soap opera popular in Brazil at the time, and on the night of January 15, 1986, the *pistoleiros* at Sete Barracas went to a neighboring land-owner's ranch to watch it. "They left a candle on top of a box in front of the house," recalled Raimunda. "The candle burned down and set the box on fire, and then the house caught fire too." By coincidence – or God's will, as some believe – this was precisely the hut where the *pistoleiros* had stored their entire stock of weapons and ammunition. "Bullets were flying everywhere, and all the weapons were destroyed. The *pistoleiros* became a little discouraged after that, packed up their things and left," Raimunda said.

Though the peasants did not immediately return to rebuild their homes, they did begin working their old plots of land during the day, and spirits were raised. Later that year, after Josimo's murder, 500 peasants, many from the Parrot's Beak, went to Brasília to demand that the government disappropriate land in areas of extreme conflict. A group of fourteen stayed for almost a month, sleeping in front of the Planalto (the Brazilian White House), and though Sarney refused to meet with them, he was ultimately forced to act. Sete Barracas, and a number of other troublespots, were disappropriated and Raimunda's family, along with thirty others (of the original fifty-two, twenty-one had left the region after being expelled the previous September) returned to their land and rebuilt their homes.

Since then, Raimunda has traveled frequently throughout the Parrot's Beak, organizing and encouraging peasants who still have no land. (Whenever a major meeting is held, Raimunda is invited along to lead events, sing, and otherwise keep things moving). She said,

It's important not to be afraid. I once went to lift the spirit of a community in an area of conflict, with a few other people from the union – a group of *posseiros* had been thrown off the land. But when we got there we discovered that the mayor and other government officials were already holding a meeting. One official got up and made a speech, telling the peasants not to go back to their land, but promising the government would take care of the situation. The mayor said something similar.

Then, I made a speech, and said the government had made us a lot of promises, but never fulfilled them – they needed to fight for the government to deliver. The mayor got up, and said, "I'd say the same thing, if I didn't think these people would be shot if they went back." And then I said, "*Companheiros*, you're the ones that know, but you can stay and fight, and risk a bullet – at least that's a quick death. Or you can wait for the government and die slowly from hunger."

Raimunda does not draw a hard and fast distinction between her work with the Base Community, the union, and the PT. "It's all part of the same struggle," she points out. And without exception, all of the local PT activists are union members. (There is no local chapter of the party, in the sense of an institutionalized structure, with a head-quarters, and so on. Meetings are held at homes, or in the large building – made of mud bricks – that serves as the union's head-quarters and assembly hall.) The work she does that is most specifi-cally party-oriented is campaigning for PT candidates, at the local and state level (and at the national level for Lula's 1989 presidential bid).

Unfortunately, the PT's lack of resources makes it difficult to run effective campaigns. In 1988, Raimunda's husband and brother were candidates – the former for vice-mayor of Itaguatins and the latter for the City Council. While they tried to cover the region by foot, sleeping overnight in the homes of sympathizers, candidates from the traditional parties drove through the area in comfortable cars, with loudspeakers mounted on top, to tell residents of their devotion to the poor. Often, they would be followed by trucks stocked with cachaça – a sugar-cane liquor somewhat similar to rum – and would occasionally hold joint campaign rallies/barbecues – a sure crowd pleaser, espe-cially as participants were liable to eat more meat at the event than they would for the next six months. Also making things difficult for any leftist party in the area is the near-feudal social relationship between peasants who do not own their own land – who form a majority – and the landowners. One woman, whose husband worked for the miser-able equivalent of $10 per month, said she intended to vote for his employer, a rich farmer, who was a candidate for state office. "We work for him, and have to go with him," she said.

Raimunda's relations both lost their bid for public office, but she believes the PT has a strong future in the Parrot's Beak, and in Brazil. "The PT is the only party that ever did anything to help us. It's a long road, but we've grown a lot here, and one day we'll be a majority," she said. (In the 1988 elections, the PT elected a total of seven city council members throughout the Parrot's Beak. One was later expelled because party members believed he had "sold out.")

Centro dos Mulatos, where Maria and her family live, along with about 1,000 other families, is 130 kilometers west of Sete Barracas. The village was named after its first president, Jośe Mulato, who arrived in 1972.

Maria is a lively woman, with an easy laugh, and extremely dedicated to the "struggle." She serves on the local union's support group (the only woman among its seven members), works with the PT (she was a candidate for City Council in 1988), the Base Community, and helped organize a woman's group in the village. She is considered "*firme*," by all who know her. Six years ago, when government officials demanded her family abandon its land in Centro dos Mulatos, she decided she'd had enough. "If you don't want us to stay on this land, you can send a *pistoleiro* to kill my husband, my children and I. If you don't do that, we're staying." They still work on the same land.

The family came to Centro dos Mulatos after having been expelled for the second time after moving to the region. Until 1977, the village was completely isolated, but that year the *posseiros* completed a narrow road that connected it to Buriti, the largest village in the area (and called "the city" by many of the local peasants, despite having a total population of no more than a few thousand people), some thirty kilometers away. "We opened the road in the morning, and in the afternoon a landowner presented himself. On the very first day! And in the very first car! He told us we were on his land, and he intended to sell it." But Maria's family, along with many others, were determined not to move again. "There was nowhere else to go, and we entered the struggle to conquer a piece of land," she said.

By 1982, after years of organizing, Maria and other activists founded a union (which later joined the CUT) – only the second in the Parrot's Beak at the time. That same year, the president, Sebastião

Batista Barbosa, was arrested by federal police, who forced him to get on his knees and pray as they viciously beat him. He left the region afterwards, but the union continued to grow. With about 1,500 members, it is one of the strongest in the Parrot's Beak.

Maria's family won title to their land back in 1983, part of the first peasant victory in the Centro dos Mulatos, but many continue to live in areas whose ownership is still in dispute. A few years ago, a landowner ordered *pistoleiros* to occupy a neighbor's plot of land. The union decided that a group of seven women, including Maria and her mother, Matilde, then sixty-three, should go to the land and work together. They planted rice under the eyes of the *pistoleiros*, who threatened them and demanded they leave. (In this case, Maria said, Brazilian machismo was helpful. If it had been men sent to work the plot, the gunmen would have been more likely to simply open fire.) The women stood their ground, and did their best to ignore the gunmen as they continued their work. "We were afraid, but we decided if we were going to die of hunger, we'd die fighting," she said.

On the following day, Vale and four other men from the village returned. Seven *pistoleiros* arrived shortly afterwards and a standoff ensued. The *pistoleiros* were heavily armed, and the peasants had only "faith in God," as Vale said. But it was the gunmen who blinked, apparently fearing there were other *posseiros* in the forest, and left the men in peace. Groups of peasants, organized by the union, continued to work the land until the *pistoleiros* stopped returning to the area.

After Josimo's murder, the government appropriated most of the disputed land in Centro dos Mulatos, for the purpose of agrarian reform. Madalena Hausser, a French nun who lives in the village, said peasants were so outraged by the priest's death that "there would have been a war" if the government had not acted. But for Maria, it was Josimo's life, not his death, that led to the victories. "With Padre Josimo, we learned to struggle. He was committed to the workers, the unions and the gospel. Without him, we wouldn't be here," she said.

Though Josimo had known his life was in danger, he refused to leave the Parrot's Beak, as many peasants and religious workers had urged him to do. "He had a place to go," said Raimunda. "But he asked, 'Where will you go? You have nowhere,' So he stayed with us."

Two weeks before he was murdered, Josimo addressed a meeting of the CPT, and the words he spoke that day appear on a poster that hangs in homes, chapels, and union halls throughout the Parrot's

Beak, often next to PT and CUT banners. "It's time to take a stand," he said. "I die for a just cause. . . . All that is happening is a logical consequence of my work, in the struggle and defense of the poor, on behalf of the gospel, that leads me to assume responsibility up to the final consequences. My life is worth nothing in view of the deaths of so many peasants, who have been assassinated, violated, thrown off their land, leaving women and children abandoned, without love, without bread, without a home."

His courage and commitment are still a driving force in the region. Every year, on May 10, peasants and religious activists hold a ceremony somewhere in the Parrot's Beak, to honor him. According to the CPT, there were forty-five major areas of conflict in the Parrot's Beak at the time of the priest's death. Little by little, the government appropriated most of those lands and gave them to the peasants who had fought so long to live there. That makes the region one of the few areas in the country that has seen more victories than defeats in the past five years.

The PT, which played an important role in those victories, has grown steadily in the region, one of its strongholds in the interior (though it is by no means a majority party in the Parrot's Beak, the party is a force to be reckoned with). When the party was formed, Lula said it did not want to take over the social movements, but serve as a vehicle to express popular demands:

> We don't need to have different manners of organizing the bases in the parties, the unions, the mass movements or in the Church. What is necessary is to develop a clear differentiation in the institutions themselves. The PT has its own program, its own documents and ideas. The PT doesn't intend to assume the tasks of the Church or of the union movement. Nor do we want to transform the Base Communities, the neighborhood associations, student groups or unions. . . . What the PT intends is to channel [the forces] of all these organizations in such a way as to conquer a nationwide projection. . . . In terms of effective organization, every sector of society should be organized; the Church and Base Communities have a specific role to play. Also the unions and neighborhood association. And the political party has its own role to bring together these organizations at a regional and national level.[14]

In the 1989 presidential elections, the PT surprised many people when it became clear that the party had gone a long way towards accomplishing that goal, and its support in the interior proved to be far stronger than anyone had thought possible just ten years earlier.

NOTES

1. Rachel Meneguello, *PT – A Formação de Um Partido 1979-1982*, p. 37.

2. By the 1980s, the Church was considered by the military to be one of the country's biggest problems. In a secret document of 1986 (leaked to the press in 1988) produced by the National Security Council, an advisory body to then president Sarney, and dominated by military officials, the CNBB was called a "serious threat to democracy." The document said that Church progressives had imposed an "essentially socio-political, not to say revolutionary, line." The document also called Church progressives "adversaries of capitalism . . . that promise the implantation of socialism, even though some euphemistically speak of an intended third path between capitalism and classic communism." The threat posed by these Church activists was so great that the Council proposed "appropriate mechanisms for the control of the activity of religious organizations in Brazil, of the participation of foreign priests and of the entrance into the country of financial resources destined for Church campaigns." *Jornal do Brasil*, August 28, 1988.

3. Sue Branford and Oriel Glock, *The Last Frontier*, p. 137.

4. Ibid., p. 138.

5. The Base Communities are looked upon warily by the Vatican. In March 1986, the Pope called twenty-one Brazilian clergymen to Rome to talk about the Church's political activities, and one of his chief concerns were the Base Communities.

6. Branford and Glock, pp. 142-3.

7. Casaldáliga continues to be controversial in recent years. In 1988, the Vatican placed restrictions on his visits to Central America (he was a strong supporter of the Sandinista government in Nicaragua, as well as leftist guerrilla movements in El Salvador and Guatemala). He was also warned about his interpretation and implementation of liberation theology. If the Vatican thought the actions would intimidate Casaldáliga, they soon learned otherwise. As *Veja* magazine noted in its October 5, 1988 issue, he not only continued speaking out but "more so than before." In the days after the press reported the warning, Casaldáliga suggested that Pope John Paul II was ignorant of Brazilian reality and was not "infallible." At about the same time an interview (that had been conducted earlier) with the Bishop was published by the Italian magazine *Jesus*, in which Casaldáliga said, "I believe that, in front of God, there exists no argument, either biological or traditional, or even theological, that impedes women from having the right to hold the same positions as men within the Church." Pope John Paul II had just been involved in a major controversy for upholding the opposite position.

In Brazil, he is criticized for more earthly matters. For example, the rich are not treated with the deference they are accustomed to in Casaldáliga's diocese. One wealthy landowner, Ricardo Perreira de Queiros, told *Veja*, "Priests here put the people against us. To have money here is a sin." One of the diocese's priests, identified by the magazine as "Mirim," refused to baptize de Queiros's 14-month old daughter Natalia, and the landowner complained the ceremony would have to be performed in a Minas Gerais parish, where he had relatives. Mirim explained the reason for his failure to attend to de Queiros: "There is a norm in the archiocese not to baptize people tied to the Rural Democratic Union [a right-wing landowners' organization]. When Natalia grows up, if she participates in the community, she'll be baptized." Another wealthy resident of the region, storeowner José Rodrigues, told *Veja*, "Until I met Bishop Pedro, I was a Catholic, but today I am no longer. I live next door to the city cathedral, but I don't want to enter in the church and be called a 'shark' [exploiter]".

8. There were other signs the landowners, certainly among the most reactionary in Latin America, would resort to drastic measures to block the reform program if the government moved forward. In 1985, a ship from Argentina was boarded by law enforcement officials in the port of Rio de Janeiro. A wide variety of heavy weaponry was found. The crew, mostly Americans, claimed the weapons were to be sold to the government of Ghana, which subsequently denied any knowledge of the shipment. It was widely believed the weapons were destined for landowner groups.

9. Campanha Nacional pela Reforma Agraria, *A Urgencia da Reforma Agraria*, June 17, 1986.

10. All quotes in this section are from interviews with the author in October 1988, unless otherwise noted.

11. Many of the CPT's activists ultimately did join the PT. Among the most important was Lourdes Lucia Goi, a nun from southern Brazil who worked closely with Josimo and whose importance to the land struggle was almost as important as the priest's. She left the Church after her order demanded she leave the region. Goi still has contact with the CPT but is more directly involved with the PT today. Another important activist, CPT lawyer Oswaldo Alencar Rocha – who filed hundreds of lawsuits seeking to defend embattled peasants – also left the organization to work more closely with the PT.

12. Gunmen are easily hired in the region. In the city of Imperatriz, two *pistolagem* agencies were openly run by prominent residents. They closed after Josimo's murder. Further south, in the city of Goiania, a gun-for-hire agency called "The Solution," founded by Irineu da Silva Mattos, a former Secretary of Public Security, offered another alternative for those with personal or political scores to settle. Police acted with as much rigor in investigating these firms as they did with the hired killers – officers only went to the site of Josimo's murder four days after he was killed. The landowners believed to have paid Rodrigues were never captured, though several appeared openly for days before disappearing.

13. *Veja*, May 21, 1986.

14. Maria Helena Moreira Alves, *Estado e Oposição no Brasil*, p. 277.

5

The Institutional Road

The PT's first public test took place during the spring 1982 elections, when, for the first time since the military coup, the people would freely choose state governors as well as national, state and municipal representatives. The election represented the completion of the initial electoral phase of the controlled process through which the dictatorship implemented the political "opening."

The PT defined its intention to participate in the electoral process in a national party conference which took place more than a year before the elections: the party would present candidates for all positions, "running on its own ticket and preserving its political independence," declared a document released at the end of the meeting.[1]

As the elections grew near, the PT held a new national conference in March 1982, and defined the nature of its participation more systematically. In an electoral charter elaborated during the convention, the context in which the elections would be held was defined as a combination of acute political crisis for a government rapidly losing legitimacy, the growth of popular movements and serious economic problems due to the economic recession which had begun at the start of the decade. Among the key demands aired at the meeting were the call for the formation of a national union headquarters, the intensification of the rural struggle and "the affirmation of a new content to the pastoral activity of the [Catholic] Church." The party believed the ability of workers to act as a "politically independent and organized force" had been greatly strengthened.[2]

Analyzing the contending forces in the electoral process, the PT

77

distinguished three camps: the government and its social base, the liberal opposition, and the working class. Party officials highlighted the government's intention to resist, by authoritarian means, its loss of control over Congress and over the means of choosing the new president of the republic. That fact was evidenced by the adoption of a series of restrictive measures concerning the rules for the year's elections. Among the most important were the government's attempt to prevent the opposition from forming coalitions by forcing voters to choose candidates of the same party for all offices, and making the formation of new parties more difficult by imposing criteria of proportionality and national representation.

The liberal opposition, embedded in the PMDB, was characterized as being totally dissociated from the PT. Its manifesto emphasized "national unity", in the interests of disenchanted sectors of the dominant classes who hoped to obtain a new correlation of forces with the military government.

For the workers, the elections represented the best opportunity since the military coup "to expand the scope of organization and political mobilization." The favorable conditions for the popular vote were a result of the political and economic crisis, which encouraged anti-government sentiment and, crucially, the possibility of voting for a party other than one of the two created by the military regime's post-coup legislation. Moreover, the PT's presence in the balloting provided for the development of a more profound political debate during the electoral campaign.

If the importance of the institutional struggle for the strengthening of the party's position was emphasized, the PT also pointed to the limitations of this struggle in one of the Charter's articles entitled, significantly, "Elections and Power," which asserted that the elections would "in no way challenge the existing political power structures." At most, the document said, they would "alter the current control of government structures at the municipal and state levels, without interfering with the decision-making centers."[3]

In its criticism of the limitations of the electoral process, the Charter did not specify whether the problem lay in the obstacles imposed by the dictatorship or in the nature of the bourgeois democratic election process. The so-called "decision-making centers," on the other hand, were clearly defined as the bureaucracy, especially state economic technocrats, the armed forces, and capital; this implies the party did have serious doubts about the electoral process itself.

The PT's objective in the campaign was to gather forces for a struggle which, it was assumed, would take place at a different, but undefined, level. Electoral participation, the document said, should serve "as a tool in the organization and mobilization of workers and the construction of popular power."[4] This position, originally formulated by Chilean radical left factions during the 1970 to 1973 Popular Unity government of Salvador Allende, is imprecise. It is valuable as a descriptive vision that points to the need for the organization of alternative power structures, but does not specifically define a strategy for the conquest of the "bourgeois" state.

This approach suggests a specific party agenda for the electoral campaign, defined in the Charter as "a stage of learning, of gathering support, of publicizing a program of transformations, of gaining a wider space for the strengthening of the workers' political organization and greater support for the social struggles."

The basic objectives of the electoral campaign were defined as follows:

1. to bring the PT's platform to the workers;
2. to become the party which would unify the workers in a program that would represent, in the struggle against the dictatorship, the interests and demands of the workers and popular movements;
3. to participate in the electoral campaign alongside labor and popular organizations, incorporating all demands made by the masses;
4. to impose an electoral defeat on the dictatorship and the forces that supported it, directly or indirectly.[5]

The party's aim, thus, was to attain propaganda and political education objectives and achieve an organic strengthening of the party, consolidate its links with mass movements and contribute to the political weakening of the dictatorship. Party activities would be concerned with demonstrating that "the only policies that are effectively oppositionist are those that express the interests of the workers."[6] The PT came under heavy attack from those who stayed in the PMDB, including many leftists, who accused the party of splitting the opposition. But party leaders responded by affirming they intended to represent the real interests of the working class, which in the PMDB were subordinated to those of the liberal bourgeoisie.

Having established these objectives, the PT decided against participating in any coalitions, even before the restrictive legislation of the military regime was decreed. If the decision made possible the PT's presence as an autonomous force, it ultimately encouraged "tactical voting" – to the great detriment of the party's candidates – opposition supporters casting their ballots for the party with the best chance of beating the military's candidates.

Despite the unanimity within the PT with respect to electoral participation – a corollary of its existence as a legal party and its commitment to institutional struggle – the document reflects a certain discomfort, which is apparent in repeated statements questioning the effectiveness of the electoral process: "The elections represent . . . merely an isolated moment within our continuing political activity, an episode in the pursuit of the final objective which is to construct a socialist society, in which there are neither exploited nor exploiters. Our participation in the electoral process cannot, therefore, serve to divert the party from its programmatic objectives."[7]

Rigorous criteria were developed for candidates in the selection process, that included nomination by the party's base, or *nucleos*, past participation in workers' movements and party-building activities; there was also a preference for candidates with a working-class background. The concern was that the list of candidates represented the social movements but also gave priority to the most active militants, whoever they might be, in order to strengthen the *nucleos*. An array of obligations was also established for candidates who won office, including rules and guidelines for their congressional activities and an obligatory donation of 40 per cent of their salary for party finances.

Although the PT ran candidates for state offices throughout the nation, emphasis was given to the campaign in São Paulo, the party's birthplace. Lula's candidacy for the governorship of the country's largest state represented the PT's major challenge. His presence on the ballot was among the most important political accomplishments by a union leader in Brazilian history, yet there were many who objected to his entry into politics and, even more, to the formation of a workers' party. (During a pre-election trip to Europe, Lula met Polish labor leader Lech Wałęsa in Rome, which contributed to loose and sometimes superficial analogies between the two, at least among some Brazilian journalists. As they noted, both were Catholic labor leaders forged in grassroots union movements against dictatorial regimes, and independent of communist parties. During the meeting, Wałęsa joined those voices advising Lula against the formation of a party and warning him not to become involved in politics. From that moment on, differences between the two became clearer and clearer, and, over time, more important.)

The major thrust of the PT's campaign was to affirm the existence, for the first time in Brazil's history, of a labor-based party, formed from the bottom up without links or alliances with the dominant sectors. The party's formulations and conceptions were mostly based on the idea of class struggle, and, as rudimentary as they may have been, served to delineate the difference between the PT and the "laborist" line which originated with Getúlio Vargas.

Lula's candidacy was based on the slogan "A Brazilian Like You," in an attempt to challenge the notion of academic *competence* – historically deemed indispensable for the exercise of power – and to struggle against the prejudices regarding the capacity of a worker to govern.[8] The theme of the campaign was made clear in Lula's standard stump speech:

> There is a division in society and it was not us who created it. The plantation house of the *latifundiário* is not the shack of the field hand. The industrialist's meal is not the gruel of the laborer. The profit of the banker is not the salary of the bank employee. The neighborhood where the large businessman lives is not the slum of the periphery, where the laborer lives. If we are socially and economically divided, how can we be politically united?[9]

The PT organized the largest rallies in São Paulo, drawing crowds of 100,000 people by the campaign's end and generating the illusion that Lula's victory was possible, if not probable. This force, nevertheless, was not realized in the overall balloting, where the "tactical vote" prevailed and many PT sympathizers voted for winning candidate Andre Franco Montoro of the PMDB, in order to defeat the military regime. Lula finished a distant fourth with about 10 per cent of the vote; statewide, the PT was only able to elect one mayor, in the ABCD city of Diadema. Especially hard to swallow was its failure to win expected victories in other proletarian cities, where it had arisen as an important union force.

At the national level, the results were equally grim: the PT obtained only 3.1 per cent of the valid votes, fewer than those legally required for registration as a party. The party's (minimal) strength was overwhelmingly concentrated in São Paulo, where it received 71.3 per cent of its overall national vote. At the federal level, the PT elected just eight members to Congress: six in São Paulo, one in Minas Gerais and one in Rio de Janeiro, all industrialized southeastern states with large urban populations.

The results came as a slap in the face to the PT and its militants. With the poor showing came an identity crisis: how could the PT be in the right, represent the working class and incorporate its electoral demands, organize the largest rallies in São Paulo, and not even win in heavily industrialized regions? The shock of losing was intensified by attacks made by the press and other parties against the PT's intention of becoming a major national political force. Many media sources confidently predicted the PT was finished, and didn't bother masking their happiness at the prospect. "PT: The great preoccupation now is to survive," said one story in the São Paulo newspaper *Jornal da Tarde*.[10] Another São Paulo daily, *O Estado de São Paulo*, one of the most conservative in the country, was exuberant at the party's poor showing. A few months after the vote, they ran a story with the headline, "After the First Test, the PT is Ending, Many Already Leaving the Party." The story, typical of many which would appear over the years, began: "Debilitated by its disturbing defeat imposed by the ballot boxes in November . . . the Workers Party is today in disarray in the majority of states and is struggling just to survive. The number of members has dropped, meetings are more and more poorly attended and defections more frequent, and even some of the party's most ardent supporters are threatening to abandon it."[11]

While the election results had disheartened many, the press was guilty of exaggeration, or perhaps wishful thinking. The nationwide mobilization for direct presidential elections, which first began gathering force in 1983, gave the PT the opportunity to expand its relatively small political space, helping organize and participating actively in the largest mass political movement Brazil had ever known. Together with other "Diretas Já!" leaders, Lula crisscrossed the country and helped attract larger and larger crowds to the campaign's events. By late 1984, when the campaign was at its peak, hundreds of thousands of supporters packed rallies in southeastern state capitals. Thanks to Lula's part in the movement, the PT broadened its image as purely a class-based party to incorporate the role of an intransigent warrior for democratic causes.

A new challenge came when the opposition failed to obtain the two-thirds majority required to pass an amendment submitted by Congressman Dante de Oliveira of the PMDB, which would have established a direct presidential vote for 1985. Despite the reversal, the PMDB and other opposition parties had an alternative strategy prepared: the regime's opponents would participate in the scheduled Electoral College vote for president, which the dictatorship promised for late 1984. The PMDB believed, rightly in the end, it would be possible for the opposition to win in the Electoral College, with the support of conservative sectors that were abandoning the military regime as the economic crisis intensified and popular opposition to the government grew. The logic seemed irrefutable: any means would be acceptable to bring an end to the dictatorship. Later, a new civilian constitution would be created – for now, the PMDB argued, the correct strategy was that which the political moment allowed: a "legitimate" election via "illegitimate" means.

For the PT, a party whose leaders had emerged from labor strikes deemed illegal by the generals and who had suffered violence and imprisonment, this route was excessively Machiavellian. (The PT did not even propose an alternative path, such as a variant of Juan Perón's 1973 ploy in Argentina, when he obliged his backers to support Héctor Cámpora in presidential elections, since he was ineligible to succeed himself. Cámpora won, soon resigned and called new elections, leading to Perón's victory by popular ballot.) After brief discussion, the PT rejected participation in the Electoral College vote, which would be conducted by the same Congress the opposition had so long denounced, and whose process represented the confiscation of the people's right to select the country's leader. (A few months before the vote a major São Paulo newspaper conducted a poll and found that a slight majority of 50.3 per cent said they opposed the Electoral College vote).[12]

With the decision came renewed isolation and attacks. The party's critics charged that if the eight votes held by the party in the Electoral College were all that was needed to elect an opposition candidate, by withholding these votes the PT would be responsible for the election of a president who would continue the policies of the dictatorship. The campaign against the PT was fierce, even after it became evident that the moderate ticket of Tancredo Neves and José Sarney would attract sufficient votes to win without the party's support. It seemed the opposition leaders were uncomfortable in adhering to a strategy so often attributed to Stalinists, specifically the adage, "The ends justify the means," a sin they would be absolved of if everyone took part.

The issue became controversial within the PT itself, especially after three of its congressional officials rebelled and announced they would vote in the Electoral College. Party leaders and militants decided, however, that the boycott was so important, and the position of those who wished to vote for Neves so unacceptable – even if the choice did not represent a commitment to his government – that a rarely used party charter clause was invoked: in an unprecedented decision, the three "dissidents" were expelled.

As discussed previously, Neves easily won in the Electoral College vote but died before he could take office, leaving Sarney to take the reins of government. The first years of his administration were extremely difficult for the PT, largely due to the isolation resulting from its highly critical stance towards the conservative transition which was clearly taking shape. While it was irrefutable that the installation of civilian government had meant important changes, it was no less true that the elements of continuity took precedence over those of rupture. Yet for the majority of the population, the "new" appeared to outweigh the old, especially as Sarney announced a series of measures, most never carried out, which promised to redistribute wealth and break up old elite power bases, most notably in rural areas. Those who espoused gradual "redemocratization" thus attempted, with some success, to portray the PT and its leftist labor allies as being narrowly sectarian, accusing them of sabotaging the country's economic and political "recovery."

In late 1985, when Sarney had completed his first six months in office, mayoral elections were held in all major cities. Six separate state and federal elections were held between 1982 and 1990, which greatly influenced the PT. The party's *nucleos* were activated and deactivated to the beat of the electoral calendar, which became their driving force. While this did not necessarily represent an adherence to "electoralism," as opposed to grassroots organizing, its organic effect upon the PT was irrefutable.

The PT's major triumph in the 1985 vote was the election of Maria Luisa Fontenelle as mayor of Fortaleza, Ceará, one of the most important northeastern state capitals – a vote which surprised even its own activists. Three years earlier, the PT's mayoral candidate in the city received just 0.9 per cent of the votes, while Fontenelle got 35 per cent. The elected mayor belonged to a Maoist faction within the PT, and she won by channeling the growing social discontent in the impoverished region into broad-based political support, despite only lukewarm enthusiasm for her campaign among most party activists. (Conflicts between the party's local directory and the mayor soon arose, and the local government proved incompetent and unable to resolve the city's major problems. Fontenelle was also undermined by the right. In the most telling demonstration of the mentality of the northeastern elite, holes suddenly began appearing in Fortaleza's streets during her tenure, with broomsticks placed in them and signs attached saying, "Here is the hole of Maria Luisa in which everyone puts their stick." In the 1988 local elections the PT's candidate received less than 5 per cent of the vote – Fontenelle had by then defected to the small Brazilian Socialist Party. Whether due to inexperience or to the negative conception of power that, from the beginning, was part of the party's orientation, the difficulties in Fortaleza demonstrated the PT's lack of preparation for assuming administrative posts. From then on, the PT was forced to view government power and the possibilities of assuming it in a different light.)

The PT's victory in Fortaleza, and its increasing, if still limited, electoral strength in other areas in the 1985 vote surprised and troubled conservatives. The period marked the onset of a major public relations campaign against the party, led by the Sarney government. Two episodes in 1986, in which the PT (or a faction of the party) was involved, gave the right its ammunition. In July 1986, a rural strike by sugar-cane migrant workers in Leme, São Paulo state was repressed by the military police, with two strikers, one a woman, killed in the violence. The PT and the CUT were immediately accused by the Justice Minister and the state governor (the PMDB's liberal Franco Montoro) of being responsible for the gunshots that led to their deaths. The accusation would doubly incriminate the PT: for possessing and using firearms and for having shot at workers it professed to be defending, which suggested the incident was an attempt to intimidate the workers and force them to participate in the mobilization. (This was similar to official United States and El Salvadoran accusations that leftist rebels in the latter country murder poor peasants, as a means of casting doubt on the "honor" of the armed forces.) Although thoroughly implausible, this version was the most widespread, largely due to its dissemination in the press. Two years went by before the courts ruled it was the military police that had opened fire on the workers, and forced the state to pay compensation to the victims' families.

In the second episode, which helped accelerate the party's explicit commitment to electoral politics, members of a clandestine group acting within the PT, and using the party for recruitment and legal cover, were arrested by police while attempting to rob a bank in Salvador, Bahia. The PT's leadership reacted immediately, denying its responsibility for the crime. Officials claimed the action was the work of infiltrators and immediately expelled the participants. Lula said in an interview at the time, in which he defended "radicalism," "I don't consider the attitude of Salvador to be radical. I consider it imbecilic. There is a big difference between imbecility and radicalism."[13] Although the leadership's action was swift, the incident provoked a certain discomfort among far-left sectors, since the PT had never defined the institutional struggle as its only sphere of action, even though it had disassociated itself from the armed struggle.[14] The right ignored the words and deeds of the leadership and said the party was entirely responsible for the hold-up. (Of course, when elected officials from the right or center were implicated in criminal activities, such as the murder of rural activists, neither the press nor the government ever tried to implicate their party in the lawlessness – the concept of collective guilt applied only to the PT.)

With Sarney having launched the infamous "Cruzado Plan" in early 1986 – which was at the zenith of its success and popularity when the Leme and Salvador incidents became nationwide issues – the government had a relatively easy time stigmatizing the PT as subversive and incapable of accepting democratic norms. *Folha de São Paulo* reported on July 20, 1986, that the National Intelligence Service had concluded that the PT and the CUT were engaged in the "destabilization of not only the government but of the capitalist system." The article reported that intelligence head Ivan Mendes believed the party wanted to "demoralize" the Cruzado Plan and open up space for "armed actions." Sarney, the newspaper reported, also subscribed to this theory. As the Cruzado Plan had won the support of the working class, the PT's actions (in addition to Leme and Salvador, the party was held accountable for every strike then being called throughout the nation) were designed to "elevate the cost of labor and jeopardize supply, two measures capable of upending the [Cruzado Plan's] price freeze."

Folha de São Paulo is by far Brazil's best newspaper, and the citation of its report is not meant to imply that it was an active participant in the smear campaign against the PT. The same cannot be said of most of the country's newspapers and other media outlets, which acted largely as the government's mouthpieces. One of the most contemptible stories, by leading "journalist" Carlos Chagas of *O Estado de São Paulo*, was headlined "Sarney Says the PT Wants Armed Struggle." Everything said in the article was attributed to Sarney but the distinction between the views of the journalist and the president was difficult to spot. The article is worth quoting because it is indicative of the hysteria and wrath towards the PT on the part of the political mainstream. Equally important is the fact that these attacks are very effective – the PT has very little access to the major media outlets and has a hard time defending itself from such accusations. According to the article, the president had concluded that the PT, frustrated by its inability to immediately score major electoral triumphs, was "despairing of conquering power by the vote [and had] opted for the path of violence and armed struggle"; the party wanted, "through social contestation [to] upset the political process," and had adopted a line of action "where the appeal to violence and confrontation is constant." Sarney pointed out, noted the spokesman/journalist, that after the PT-linked bank robbers were arrested in Salvador, "this type of assault dropped by 50 per cent throughout the country. Coincidence or evidence that, until then, elements linked to the PT were given to such practices?" (The very dubious accuracy of the 50 per cent figure cited by Sarney was accepted at face value by Chagas.) As to Leme, Chagas pondered – via Sarney – "What were they [PT elected officials] doing there, in the middle of the night? Hunting birds?"[15]

This entire debate was taking place, conveniently for the right, as the November 1986 gubernatorial and congressional elections were coming up. The vote was crucial because the Congress to be selected would first serve as a Constituent Assembly and write a new constitution, establishing the framework for civilian rule.[16] Early in the year, it appeared the PT (and other opposition sectors, notably Leonel Brizola's PDT) might advance significantly, as the reformist and democratizing impetus of Sarney's administration was losing force and revealing its limitations. But with the public relations campaign concerning the PT's alleged anti-social proclivities and the apparent success of Sarney's economic emergency program, prospects rapidly dimmed.

The PT and the PDT, as well as the CUT, had been opposed to the Cruzado Plan from the start. The unions fought, with little success, against the immediate wage losses the plan caused by freezing both high prices and eroded wages. The argument that "the best way to defend wages is to eliminate inflation" gained sway, as did the call for workers to forget past losses and concentrate on later gains obtained with inflation "under control." The left also criticized the government for not declaring a moratorium on the foreign debt, which its leaders said was crucial to the long-term success of any program of economic stabilization. (This assessment proved to be accurate. In early 1987, after the Cruzado Plan had been quietly abandoned, Sarney was forced to call an apolitical moratorium on Brazil's commercial debt, arguing that the country simply did not have sufficient foreign reserves to make payments. But by then, with the economy once again reeling, the country had no bargaining power with its creditors and was able to obtain no concessions from private lenders.) Finally, leftists questioned Sarney's long-term commitment to implementing promised structural reforms, as he was surrounded by political and military figures closely identified with the status quo.

But the plan's popularity during its first months, as discussed in Chapter 3, was overwhelming and the PT's criticism looked like mere political posturing for the November elections. Candidates from the PMDB and the PFL, which formed the pro-government Democratic Alliance, campaigned on the success of the Cruzado Plan and Sarney helped by vowing to maintain the price freeze until inflation was forever eliminated. The result was the previously mentioned PMDB-PFL landslide.

Despite the Cruzado Plan's broad coat-tails, the PT was able to triple its congressional seats to eighteen. A comparison of overall election results in 1982 with those of 1986 shows that votes for the PT increased from 3 to 7 per cent, rising from nearly 1.5 million to 3.5 million. (This would have given it thirty-four seats in Congress if the number of representatives elected corresponded to the percentage of votes received nationally, instead of being doled out on a state-by-state basis. The discrepancy resulted from the fact that the industrial states of the southeast, where the PT, and the left in general, is strongest, are under-represented in Congress, helping maintain the national power of the reactionary elite of the more conservative and more sparsely populated north and northeast.) The party also increased from three to seven the number of states where it elected at least one federal congressman. The number of state legislatures where the party was represented grew from three to thirteen – that is, half of the nation's states or territories. The most spectacular success, though, was Lula's massive support in São Paulo, where he received 656,000 votes, more than any other federal congressman in the country.

The PT was growing, but always below the expectations of its activists and supporters. The dynamic of growth collided head on with the fact that an immense sector of the population had been left economically abandoned by Brazilian peripheral capitalism. The intermittent employment and marginalization of the majority make their capacity for organization, political consciousness and collective action far more difficult. Furthermore, the media's ability to control the flow of information is tremendous and the degree of popular "de-politicization" is great. Under these conditions, the PT and the CUT were frequently isolated, even after the Sarney government abandoned the Cruzado Plan. His decision provoked widespread anger, but led to more apathy than it did revolt. For the small middle class, civilian rule had produced important changes, especially the intangible benefits resulting from increased civil and political liberties. They were outraged by the government's turnaround and have vehicles, especially the press, to express their anger. For the poor, though, who are far more concerned with food on the table than a free press, the government's betrayal of the economic emergency plan made it seem as if little had changed from the days of the dictatorship; the political system and political parties in general were thus largely discredited. (The well-known Brazilian adage that politicians are all "flour from the same sack" was repeated endlessly at the time.) Both the PT's and the CUT's cadres are overwhelmingly drawn from organized, politi-cized and activist sectors of the population. With despair and cynicism abundant in the post-Cruzado Plan period, the left had a hard time motivating its cadres.

This isolation was witnessed, and heightened, during the proceed-ings of the Constitutional Assembly, which convened on February 1, 1987. The PT participated in the Assembly with a project of its own, but was forced to seek propaganda victories as opposed to concrete ones, since the party had only 18 deputies out of a total of 570 (overall the left held a distinct minority of seats). In its introduction, the PT's constitutional proposal stated that it would seek to "speak for the interests it represents, formulating a proposal for the whole of society based upon the wishes and demands that arise from those who constitute our party's reason for existence: the rural and city workers."[17] The PT declared that it based its conception of a truly democratic society upon two fundamental pillars: the restoration of individual rights and guarantees and popular control of public power.

In a chapter titled "The Origins and Purposes of Power," the PT affirmed that the new charter should defend the principle of popular sovereignty, reiterating that power should be exercised by delegations and direct participation. Also called for was the people's right to revolt against authoritative acts which violated rights guaranteed by the (new) charter, and the definition of mechanisms which would allow for public control through extralegal popular councils.

As the sole party with a long-standing presence in the popular movements, the PT participated heavily in the debate's early phase, presenting their demands. Some important victories were scored during the constitutional debate. These included the unconditional right to strike (later watered down by a bill in Congress), 120-day paid maternity leave (and five days' paternity leave), a six-hour maximum uninterrupted work shift, increased dismissal compensation, and the extension of full labor rights to maids and other domestic workers.[18]

However, these victories stirred the right into action. Army Minister Pires warned that "an active, disciplined minority" was running amok. Soon, conservatives formed a bloc in the Assembly that became known as the "*centrão*," or Big Center, and which seized control of the debate. (The military itself set up a group of officers, euphemistically called "parliamentary counselors," who acted as permanent lobbyists.) Among their key aims was to defeat a left proposal to limit Sarney's term to four years; a proposal which was favored, according to public opinion polls, by about 80 per cent of the population and which would have resulted in presidential elections being held in 1988. That, it was thought, would benefit left candidates, due to the country's deepening economic troubles. It appeared the proposal would pass before Sarney's troubleshooters, without troubling to cover their tracks, began doling out concessions for TV and radio stations, plots of land, and reportedly direct cash payments, as a means of swaying legislators. Military officials also warned Assembly members that a 1988 election was unacceptable. The Congress promptly caved in and Sarney got his five-year term.

Another key issue was the question of the military's right to intervene in domestic affairs. PT Deputy José Genoíno managed to get an Assembly committee to draft a clause limiting the role of the armed forces to external defense. The ubiquitous Army Minister quickly rose to the challenge, publicly announcing that the armed forces wanted to "keep intact their prerogative of intervening in the running of the republic when they judge constitutional powers or law and order to be in danger."[19] His wishes were heeded. The Assembly agreed the generals could intervene in "defending the law and public order," the only restriction being that such activity had to be requested by one of the three branches of government. Also defeated were proposals to create a joint Defense Ministry or demilitarize the National Intelligence Service. The constitution also said that the military police (state troopers), which are subordinated to state governments, can be put under army control at times of crisis. Other defeats for the PT and the left included, in addition to the painful loss on agrarian reform (discussed in Chapter 4), a negative vote on a proposal that would have required that national plebiscites be held on important issues facing the country (such as payment on the foreign debt) and the continued existence of the "Union Tax," deducted from workers' pay to finance the populist labor system.[20]

After the left's defeat on these, and many other important measures, the PT decided to sign the new charter but vote "no" in the Assembly when the final document was called up to be approved or denied. (It was the only party to do so.) The party also decided to publicly denounce the conservative character of the charter and point out its many shortcomings. After congressional debate had largely been concluded, the PT released a "Circular From the National Directory," which read in part:

> The PT, as a party that supports socialism, is by nature opposed to the bourgeois order, the foundation of capitalism. Thus, the PT rejects the bourgeois constitution that will be promulgated . . . [the party] rejects the immense majority of its laws which constitute the institutionalization of the bourgeois order that the party seeks to destroy and, in its place, construct a socialist society.
>
> However, the PT has to carry out its activities – the political expression of the class struggle – where the real battle takes place, and not in imaginary or artificial forums. . . . In the specific case of the constitution, all of the PT's activities expressed [an] anti-institutional struggle from inside the institution. . . . [In many instances] the PT's block of deputies was forced to choose the option that was least unpleasant. . . . [The party] saw the Congress as an area of struggle and in it sought to act in accord with its programmatic principles.
>
> [But] the PT does not denounce the new constitution because it is a party that favors socialism and the new charter configures a capitalist society. The PT was always aware that at this historic moment, with the existing correlation of forces and at the actual stage of class struggle, there is no possibility of creating a socialist society in Brazil, much less through this

Congress. For this reason, the party's constitutional program did not propose a socialist society, but a package of principles and mechanisms capable of broadening democratic spaces and popular participation in the political process, though still within a capitalist framework.

The principal reason for the PT's attitude of repudiation, rejection, criticism and protest towards the constitution that will soon be promulgated is that even within the strict limits of a capitalist society the new charter could have been much more democratic and popular, if not for the actions of conservative and reactionary forces that pressured the Congress: the Sarney government, the military, the large landowners, the bankers, the multinationals, the Rural Democratic Union, the *centrão*, the backward forces of all types.

Despite everything, and thanks to the force and mobilization of part of the population and progressive parties and politicians, the text of the new charter . . . contains some small victories, a few small conquests, some minimum rights for workers. Such victories and conquests, however, do not eliminate the essentially conservative, anti-democratic and anti-popular character of the constitution. For this reason, the national directory has decided that the PT will make concrete its position . . . by voting "no" to the new charter. . . .

The PT [is voicing its views] in order to avoid manipulation by other political forces. In the same spirit, the PT will seek to capitalize politically on aspects of the constitution favorable to the working class and the people, as well as identify those responsible for the unfavorable or negative aspects.[21]

The PT's attitude produced a new storm of criticism from the press and other parties, who again accused it of being excessively sectarian and radical. Once more, the PT was labelled as being an opponent of democracy, mostly by those who had unabashedly supported the old military dictatorship.

Another crucial event in terms of the party's ideological definition took place while the constitutional debate was raging, when the PT held its Fifth National Party Conference in December 1987. At the meeting, leaders reviewed political questions in light of the party's past and in view of upcoming events, specifically the 1988 local elections and the 1989 balloting for the presidency (the latter was seen as especially decisive for Brazil's future, as it would be the first direct presidential election since before the coup). The document approved at the conference – which discussed socialism as the PT's strategic objective, tactics and policies of party alliances, union orientation, and problems of internal structure – was the party's most important text ever. For the first time, the PT called for the organization of an alternative hegemony, grouping together forces in a democratic and popular platform, which was considered to be a first step toward the direct struggle for socialism. The election manifesto approved at the meeting proposed the radical democratization of the state and Brazilian society, benefiting social groups adversely affected by the process of monopolization and marginalization produced by capitalist accumulation. It included, among other measures: agrarian, urban, tax and administrative reforms; a call for severing ties with the IMF; the reduction of the foreign debt via a moratorium; measures to control capital flight; state investments in social programs; nationalization of public transportation as well as the pharmaceutical, cement and financial sectors; a forty-hour working week; and a reassessment of a nuclear program developed by the military governments, in conjunction with the West German government and Western multinationals.[22]

The PT's major concern, though, was the question of defining its future project. Ever since being founded, the party had a strong anti-capitalist orientation and identified socialism as a form of workers' self-government and self-emancipation. However, a class-based analysis had not led to the drafting of an explicit program. The party's anti-capitalism resided purely in an attack on private ownership of the means of production, workers' exploitation and social polarization. Initially, the party identified closely with Poland's Solidarity movement and, based on that, strongly criticized Eastern European regimes. (It was only at a later stage that the PT began to redefine its international profile, stressing relationships with other Latin America countries, and expressing solidarity with Cuba and Nicaragua. Subsequent contacts with Eastern European union leaders and working-class CP members, especially in the USSR, East Germany and Czechoslovakia, led to an appreciation of these countries' social accomplishments and exchanges with Eastern bloc communist parties were established.)

The document drafted at the Fifth Conference defined more specifically the type of socialism the party envisaged and how it would be implemented. Two continuous, but distinct, strategic phases were defined in the struggle for socialism: that of taking political power and that of building a socialist society.

As a precondition for taking power, said the document, "the

workers must become a hegemonic class and dominate state power,"
since "there is no historical example of a class that has transformed
society without placing political power – the State – at its service."[23]
The document viewed political organization as taking place not just at
the level of electoral campaigning but as part of the day-to-day
struggle. The fundamental forms of basic organization the party's
activists should be involved in were "those born of workers' self-
organization, the struggle for worker control of the shop floor
(through the formation of factory commissions) and of popular
control of neighbourhoods. These embryonic forms of proletarian
power are schools for self-organization and workers' political participation which aim at the construction of an effectively democratic
socialism, where power is exercised by workers themselves and not in
their name."

The party viewed these forms of organization as being instrumental
in the preparation of the working class for taking power and building a
new society. The actual means of constructing that new society was
still left unclear: there is simply a condemnation of the struggle for
piecemeal reforms when they are an end in themselves. If
"reformism" served to educate the masses and demonstrated that the
consolidation of structural change would only be possible when
workers established their own power, though, it contributed to the
struggle for social transformation and was legitimate.

The next question the document addressed was that of alliances.
The bourgeoisie was recognized as the principal enemy, in a purely
instinctive way, but it was recognized that there was a need to
differentiate between large-scale capital and small rural and urban
businessmen, emphasizing the profound disparity between the two
and the potential of incorporating the latter into the struggle for
socialism. At the same time, the document stressed the necessity of
identifying internal contradictions within the bourgeoisie that would
permit tactical alliances with some of its sectors.

After defining these strategies in the struggle for power, the document moved on to a discussion of the construction of a future society,
saying the internal development of capitalism during the previous
three decades had created a strong foundation for the establishment of
a solid socialist sector in the economy. Large agro-industrial, commercial, industrial and banking enterprises were candidates for
"immediate transformation into socialist, state or collective enterprises." Alongside these firms, the document noted, was another vast

sector of the economy which, though largely subordinated to large-scale capital, absorbed an enormous quantity of labor while providing services that were considered secondary and not highly profitable. Consisting of millions of small firms and freelance workers, this sector played an important role in the Brazilian economy and should continue to exist, even after the establishment of socialism. The magnitude of "the state or collectively owned socialist sector" needed to be clearly defined so that smaller-scale capital would be allowed to develop to a certain level, at which point it would be socialized as well. The PT did not, however, envisage a country where the economy was completely nationalized. (For example, in a 1985 interview Lula said, "I've been to Cuba and there all the bars are state-controlled, as are the taxis. I think that's a lot of responsibility for the state.")[24] Party economists also foresaw a substantial degree of private ownership in the agricultural sector, with a large number of small-scale farmers. That view probably stemmed at least partly from the experiences of PT militants in rural areas. Most Pastoral Land Commission activists interviewed in the Parrot's Beak region said they had initially promoted cooperative farming but most peasants were not enthusiastic. They wisely chose to respect that preference, instead organizing collective projects for irrigation, vegetable gardens and other community enterprises, which were quite successful. In other areas, communal landholding is not only accepted but preferred. In the northwest Amazon, rubber-tappers – almost all of them PT militants or supporters – in recent years have sought to create "extractivist reserves," in order to develop the Amazon rainforest without destroying it. The reserve lands are not owned by anyone, but the tappers have usufruct rights, collecting rubber, fruits and nuts and carrying out small agricultural projects.

The persistence of different classes and social groups during the process of constructing socialism made it necessary to recognize the existence of different political needs. Democracy was not understood to be a "concession," but "a component part in an ongoing revolution and a decisive factor in the battle against bureaucratization." The document stressed that "the absence of democracy, of the workers' right to freely organize, contradicts the socialism we are struggling for," and emphatically declared: "The PT rejects the bureaucratic concept of socialism, the vision of a single-party system, because it considers incorrect the idea that each social class is represented by a sole party." For that reason, the socialist project "should incorporate the perspectives developed by different social movements struggling against specific forms of oppression, such as women, blacks, youth and homosexuals. . . . Their ideological positions, particularly feminism, [are] indispensable for toppling important pillars of domination exercised by the bourgeoisie and for involving the majority of the Brazilian population in a process of revolutionary transformation." Socialism, it was stated, should also incorporate cultural and environmental movements, "barring their utilization by the bourgeoisie, who strip them of their critical character."

The PT's ideological debates may not have been closely followed by anyone other than its own activists and leftist intellectuals. But the party's outspoken explicitly socialist views marked it in the minds of the public as being the principal opponent of the status quo as represented by the Sarney government. And in its final two years in office, that government was almost completely discredited.

Two major anti-inflationary programs were announced in the post-Cruzado Plan period, and each had the same outcome: the cost of living slowed for several months before renewing its upward climb. Inflation for 1988 was close to 1,000 per cent, a historical high, and wreaked havoc for all but the wealthiest. Between 1986 and early 1989, three different national currencies were used. A *Wall Street Journal* article from the period captured the sense of chaos:

> "Take a banana," says Italo Gasparini, the director of the Brazilian Central Bank's currency department. "What does it cost? One hundred cruzados? Is that cheap or expensive? I don't know? Do you know?"
>
> Nobody knows. Inflation is so high, that it perplexes everyone. A television set costing 20,000 cruzados at the beginning of this year now [11 months later] costs about 190,000 ($320). Rents have been leaping more than 800 per cent a year. A newspaper may double in price overnight. The 10-cruzado bank note, worth nearly a dollar two years ago, is now routinely discarded as trash.
>
> The bank note's disgrace upsets Mr Gasparini. He recently returned from a ceremony launching the 10,000-cruzado note. When planning the note eight months ago, he hoped it would be worth $50. It buys $17. Because the ceremony started late, people joked he would have to present a 20,000-cruzado note.

The article's author, Roger Cohen, noted that poor Brazilians at the time were forced to take their wages and immediately head to the supermarket to buy supplies. If they waited long, their cruzados were worthless.[25]

With salaries continuously eroded by inflation, political and social discontent mounted. In July 1987, Rio bus fares were raised by 50 per cent, provoking violent street demonstrations and riots. Buses were burned and stones thrown and the army was finally called in when police proved unable to control crowds. At about the same time, a group of poor people near São Paulo were involved in a battle with garbage collectors over the trash. During a trip to Rio, stick-wielding, stone-throwing protestors attacked Sarney's vehicle and managed to break a few windows (in what officials tried to portray as an assassination attempt). After nearly two years of relative quiet, union groups and the popular movement again stirred. Huge strikes were called by important unions tied to the CUT, representing such groups as petroleum and dock workers. In a major show of force, army units occupied refineries and ports to crush the movements.

This quiet accumulation of forces exploded in the elections of November 1988 (the last in which executive posts would be determined in a single round balloting. From that point on, all future mayors, governors and presidents had to win an absolute majority of the votes; if such a majority was not obtained in a first round vote between all candidates, the top two vote-getters were to meet in a runoff election). The balloting took place at the tail end of a wave of strikes and demonstrations which had met with repression from both the federal and various state governments. The most violent conflict, and certainly the one that had the greatest impact on the elections, took place when army troops invaded the National Steel Company plant in Volta Redonda, ninety miles northwest of Rio, to break up a strike by metalworkers. Three workers were killed in the attack, which was carried out shortly before the vote and produced a huge voter backlash against conservative candidates. (No one from the armed forces was punished, or even reprimanded, for the action. Army Minister Leônidas Pires, who apparently ordered the invasion without consulting Sarney, even considered honoring the troops who took part in the attack; on that score, he finally backed down, realizing that he might be going a bit too far.)

The PT was closely involved in the strikes and demonstrations taking place in the months leading up to the vote, and broadcast campaign spots on television and radio that voiced support for the movements and denounced the repression. In the last two weeks of the campaign, polls began to show increasing support for the party's candidates across the country. No one, however, was prepared for the results, which represented the greatest electoral shock in the country's history: the PT won mayoral office in thirty-six (mostly major) cities, which together produce around 30 per cent of GNP. Most impressive of all were triumphs in São Paulo, South America's largest city with more than fifteen million inhabitants; Campinas, the state's second largest city; Santos, Brazil's largest port, where Telma de Souza, a professor and daughter of communist dockworkers was elected; and two key state capitals, Vitória, in the southeast, and Porto Alegre, in the extreme south of the country. The PT also swept almost all of the labor belt district surrounding São Paulo and a number of important industrial cities in Minas Gerais, the country's second most populous state.

In São Paulo, the party's winning mayoral candidate was a woman who had immigrated from the poor northeast. In the early 1960s, even before the military coup, Luiza Erundina had participated in political mobilization and literacy movements as a young teacher under the direction of educator Paulo Freire, author of the famous book, *Pedagogy of the Oppressed*. She later earned a degree in social work from a São Paulo university and became deeply involved in movements in support of the homeless. Erundina also participated in the founding of the PT, was elected to the city council and later became a state deputy. She won the party's nomination over Plínio Sampaio, a party moderate who had been favored by most key leaders, including Lula, because he was considered more electorally viable.

During her campaign's early days, Erundina presented a radical platform, which proposed the adoption of the Leninist model of "dual power" in the city's administration, as a means of preventing a PT government from being imprisoned by existing bourgeois power structures. Polls gave her almost no chance against rightist Paulo Maluf (the loser in the 1984 Electoral College vote), and several other centrist candidates who appeared well ahead of her.

But Erundina rose rapidly in the polls during the campaign's final days. For the first time ever, the "tactical vote" favored the PT, as many São Paulo residents were prepared to vote for anyone capable of beating Maluf. On election day, the PT threw thousands of activists on to the streets in an attempt to win over the undecided vote. That helped Erundina win 30 per cent of the votes, defeating Maluf by a narrow margin. The effect was stunning – as her triumph was roughly comparable to the election of a radical Algerian as mayor of Paris: a woman, and militant of the country's most radical party, would rule the continent's most advanced and sophisticated capitalist industrial park.

The PT also elected more than 1,000 city council members nation-wide (up from only 179 in the 1985 balloting), of whom close to 40 per cent were rural workers and activists, many involved in Church-supported movements. For the first time in Brazilian history, this important sector of the population would be directly represented in politics on a large scale. Overall, the PT won 28.8 per cent of the vote in Brazil's 100 largest cities (containing 38 per cent of the entire population), leaving the PMDB in second place with 18.4 per cent. Compared with mayoral elections in state capitals held three years earlier, votes for the PT rose from 1.5 million to 2.8 million, while votes for the PMDB dropped from 4.1 million to 2.4 million. Leonel Brizola's PDT also saw its support fall, from 1.7 million to 1.5 million votes.

The 1988 vote represented, to a certain extent, a protest vote channeled by the PT, and not simply an increase in the party's political following. But the isolation to which the party had been relegated since its refusal to participate in the 1984 Electoral College vote had been decisively shattered.

The elections also served to mark the definitive crisis of the PMDB, and other sectors that had played the leading roles in the transition process. The 1988 vote largely went to those parties that, in one form or another, had rejected the Sarney government and its allies. (Even the rightist vote had a populist character, as many conservative candidates sharply attacked the government during the campaign.)

However, the PT soon faced new and serious problems. Because the party had failed to fully define a strategy for exercising power, incoming mayors had difficulties administering the cities they con-trolled. The situation was made more difficult by the general weaken-ing of the state's capacity, at a regional and national level, to foster policies of social transformation – a direct result of the country's ongoing economic crisis. The PT's own classism collided with the *public* nature of those administrations as well. Practice revealed the necessity of defining strategies, and revealed a theoretical backward-ness in relation to the party's electoral success.

The next chapter in the party's electoral trajectory – the 1989 presidential vote – confirmed that the party's rapid move toward the pinnacle of the political system had taken place before it had resolved central problems concerning its definition as a revolutionary party operating within a bourgeois institutional framework with the express project of installing a new political system, socialism.

NOTES

1. Moacir Gadotti and Otaviano Pereira, *Pra Que PT*, Cortez Editora, São Paulo 1989, p. 239.
2. Ibid., p. 231.
3. Ibid., p. 233.
4. Ibid., p. 233.
5. Ibid., pp. 233–4.
6. Ibid., pp. 233–4.
7. Ibid., p. 235.
8. This stemmed largely from an innate and deeply rooted elitism on the part of Brazil's upper classes, both left and right, which was very definitely absorbed by the lower classes as well. In an interview a few years after the PT was founded, Fernando Henrique Cardoso, a highly respected leftist intellectual in the PMDB, pointed to Lula as one of the country's leading new political figures. But in follow-up comments he said, "He's really more of a mass leader than a political leader, because he always slips in his strategic vision. Lula would be better if he had followed his impulses and left aside his theoretical glasses." *Playboy*, September 1984, p. 32.
9. Gadotti and Pereira, p. 247.
10. *Jornal da Tarde*, April 18, 1983, p. 15.
11. *O Estado de São Paulo*, May 1, 1983, p. 4.
12. *Folha de São Paulo*, July 9, 1984, p. 5.
13. *Folha de São Paulo*, July 16, 1986, p. 16.
14. The PT had a few months previously been involved in a major public dispute about the question of armed struggle, after Lula gave a lengthy interview to *Folha de São Paulo* in December 1985. The headline to the story was "Lula admits armed struggle necessary to guarantee power." The relevant passage from the interview was the following:

> Lula: Look, the revolution is not determined by who defends socialism, at times it's determined by who defends capitalism. Do you think economic power and the dominant classes are going to permit the PT to win, through elections, the governorship of the state of São Paulo?
> *Folha*: I believe that depends on the degree of the strength of democracy . . .
> Lula: Right! . . . It's exactly because I have doubts . . . that I think we need to be prepared to not allow, at any moment, a retrocession by force. . . . [I accept] even that the right can win an election through the direct vote. . . . But I can't allow that the right maintains itself in power through the use of arms. Then I would be completely favorable to a resistance by the population.
> *Folha*: Equally armed?
> Lula: Equally armed. Look, that's no novelty. The American constitution, in the 1700s, allowed that, in the measure regarding the need for self-defense, to guarantee the people's will, that armed struggle was acceptable.

While Lula obviously didn't believe at the time that the left could take power via the ballot box, the interview at the end of this book makes clear that he does believe so today.

15. *O Estado de São Paulo*, July 19, 1986, p. 5.

16. A PT-supported proposal to hold separate elections, one for Congress and the governors and another for the Constitutional Assembly and state governorships had previously been defeated, thanks largely to "no" votes from the pro-government parties. The proposal emphasized the special importance of writing the new constitution, and warned that key constitutional questions would be lost in the personality-based campaigns for governor and Congress. That is precisely what happened, which worked against those who sought to politicize the debate.

17. Gadotti and Pereira, p. 301.

18. A whole series of constitutional guarantees of social and economic rights were included in the constitution, that if actually abided by would make Brazil the Sweden of Latin America. In fact, they are almost completely ignored. A few examples include a minimum salary that guarantees "basic human needs" (the minimum wage in September 1990 was worth about $60 per month, which was not even sufficient to buy the "basic basket" of foodstuffs and supplies necessary to support a family of four – not to mention covering rent, clothing, medical care, etc.); a ban on torture (which is absolutely routine for "common criminals," though eliminated otherwise); the protection of children from exploitation, violence and cruelty (an Amnesty International report from 1990 revealed the country's death squads, which operate in great measure against youths involved in drug trafficking and petty crime in urban slums, kill on average more than one adolescent per day); and a provision making racism a crime punishable by prison time (which police and judges did not take seriously – two years after the constitution was passed no one had yet served a prison term for the crime of racism).

19. Vittorio Bacchetta, *Brazil: Generals defend military powers under civilian government*, Latinamerica Press, June 25, 1987.

20. New president Fernando Collor de Mello ended the "Union Tax" in 1990, one of the few measures he decreed that had the support of the left.

21. One attempt by the CUT to identify the politicians that voted with the *centrão* in the assembly met with immediate repression. The labor federation printed a poster with photos of congressional representatives who had voted for a five-year term for Sarney, and identified them as "Traitors of the People." Federal police invaded the office where the poster was being printed, confiscated copies and acted to prevent its distribution.

22. The nuclear program was a tremendous flop in all regards, even if one chooses to ignore the issue of the preferred use of alternative energy sources. Technocrats decided to build three nuclear reactors near Angra dos Reis, a small coastal resort city located between Rio and São Paulo, the country's two largest urban centers. Billions of dollars were spent but only one reactor ever produced electricity, and it shut down so frequently Brazilians called it the "lightning bug." Well-placed sources have also charged that Brazilian officials, both before and after the return of civilian rule, cooperated with President Saddam Hussein's Iraqi regime in attempting to build nuclear weapons. In 1981, in the most notorious incident, a cargo plane reportedly took off from São Jose dos Campos, in São Paulo state, carrying two fifty-five-gallon drums of "yellow cake," enriched uranium necessary for nuclear bomb production. Local and international press accounts said the plane was forced down over Africa by Israeli pilots, who off-loaded the material before allowing the plane to continue on its way.

23. All quotes this section cited in Gadotti and Pereira, pp. 132–8.

24. *Folha de São Paulo*, December 29, 1985, p. 5.

25. Roger Cohen, "Brazil's Price Spiral Nears Hyperinflation, Could Ruin Economy," *Wall Street Journal*, December 8, 1988.

6

PT Ideology

I don't want to be the owner of the truth, I want to place my ideas in debate, so that society and principally the working class can decide what it wants.
Lula, *Folha de São Paulo*, December 29, 1985

During the first fifteen years of the dictatorship, the regime's institutional foes were largely forced to work within the MDB, or in the social movements supported by groups within the MDB. This helped to hide the very real ideological divergences between different sectors of the opposition. These distinctions became clear when the labor strikes of the late 1970s demonstrated the strength of the union movement and, at the same time, created a social base of support for a different kind of opposition to the dictatorship.

The main reason for the formation of the PT was simply that, for the first time ever, the workers' movement was capable of constructing its own political vehicle: "A party without bosses," "If we can work, we can lead," "Vote PT, the rest is bourgeoisie," "Workers vote for workers" – these slogans corresponded to the PT's phase of self-identification on the nation's political stage.

The PT began organizing without a programmatic or strategic platform. In a general sense, socialism was always a principal demand, just as the working-class – especially industrial workers – was considered to be the political vanguard. That latter concept was central, and expressed the essence of the PT's program; the party's desired social composition was, hence clearer than its platform. In a country like Brazil, where the union movement had long been dominated by

Vargas's populism, where a social-democratic tradition did not exist, where communists had little strength in the labor movement, and rarely challenged populist tenets when they did, the call for the political autonomy of the working class was enough to make the PT's project unique.

The new party's call for workers' self-emancipation became better defined as the grassroots union movement developed, and struggled, under the military dictatorship. Despite police repression of demonstrations, the arrest of leaders and massive state intervention in labor affairs, class-based union activities created the political space necessary for the PT's birth and growth. From the very start, class-based unionism opposed the labor legislation inherited from Vargas, which subordinated unions to the Ministry of Labor. The struggle for autonomy from the State during the dictatorship formed part of a general struggle on the part of civil society to obtain full rights of citizenship and self-organization. Among those involved in this struggle were women, blacks, Indians, students, artists, journalists, intellectuals, lawyers and human rights organizations, including those tied to the Church.

The attempt to stitch together a party from such diverse social movements and sectors was the PT's main novelty as a political force. In Brazil, and in Latin America in general, left parties typically followed the opposite path, with very little success. These parties were ideologically influenced by the European labor movement or, more often, by the Communist Internationals, its parties and sects. They inherited their programs from these sources, and programmatic definitions often took precedence over, and preceded chronologically, the construction of a solid social base.

In Latin America, even among the communist parties, few political parties represented a significant social base or conquered their own political space. The Uruguayan and Chilean communist parties were exceptions in successfully forming a solid labor base (which has recently been threatened by transformations in those countries' political systems engendered by the democratic transitions, as well as the ideological crisis resulting from the fall of Eastern European regimes). Other leftist parties, with the obvious exception of the Cuban Communist Party, which was formed by forces essentially outside the international communist movement, never gained a significant national presence in their respective countries.

Trotskyite and Maoist ideological tendencies survived in the region, without ever becoming important social forces anywhere on the continent. Guerrilla movements in Cuba, Nicaragua, El Salvador and Guatemala, on the other hand, were able to evolve from closed political groupings into mass movements. In these countries, political options for the left remain open; in those where the social structure, experience prior to armed movements, or the correlation of military forces points to another strategic direction, the PT's experience and growth is wholly innovative.

The crisis of the Latin American left existed, and was reaching a critical stage, even before the collapse of Eastern Europe's communist governments. In countries such as Argentina, Uruguay, Chile and Brazil, which experienced similar forms of military rule, the left emerged debilitated from the period of dictatorship. While important socialist and communist parties survived in Chile and Uruguay, their historical alliances no longer existed, which further isolated the left. In Argentina, the elimination of guerrilla organizations did not allow for the renovation of the left.

In Brazil, the left was blessed with the privilege of "lateness," or rather with advantages resulting from its renewal after a complete rupture with past progressive forces. The earlier defeat of the Brazilian left was "precocious" in comparison with other Latin American countries, in both the timing of the 1964 military coup and the defeat of anti-government armed movements a few years later. At the same time, the post-coup process of capitalist expansion led to the birth of social forces capable of generating a resurgence of progressive forces.

Born of the most technologically developed centers of Brazilian industry, with a grassroots form of organization entirely different from the official union structure, the PT brought together diverse political and ideological sectors, unified by their radical resistance to the State and capitalism. In addition to the union base that remains at the party's core are the Christian Base Communities and other Church organizations (such as the CPT, homeless and youth movements), which while not officially tied to the PT, often express themselves politically through the party. The PT also includes radical intellectuals, of Marxist or Marxist-inspired tendencies, ex-militants of 1960s guerrilla groups, human rights and civil rights activists, and Trotskyite and Maoist groups.

The coexistence of this mixture of ideologies, orientations and practices is not always peaceful. The hegemony of Lula's sector of the party, known as the "Articulation" (*Articulação*), allows for differences to be resolved, as a last resort, by an elected directorate. On various occasions, however, this directorate has been in the minority, whether in the choice of an electoral candidate or in the question of constructing alliances with other parties. Conflicts have most often arisen at a statewide level, since the dominance of the "Articulation" is securely established only at the national level. The competing forces inside the party make the PT's internal decision-making process extremely hectic. Public battles between factions and a large number of policy proposals floated at meetings sometimes project an image of organizational chaos.

However, there is a logic to this apparent chaos: wide internal democracy allows for a broad degree of divergence and autonomy. For example, the CUT is the undisputed, and intransigent, leader of innumerable strikes conducted by municipal employees against city governments where the PT itself holds power – even though these employees have higher salaries than their counterparts elsewhere. The PT's internal democracy also allowed for, and survived, a 1990 decision to end "double militancy," typical of doctrinaire organizations, whereby factions within the party maintained separate internal discipline, newspapers and finances while using the PT as a vehicle for mass organization and ideological struggle (in the old style of infiltration developed by Trotskyite groups). The PT's leadership demands that all members view the building of the party as a sui generis strategic experiment, elaborated by a network of militants in accordance with their social and political experiences, as the only means of overcoming current obstacles in traditional efforts to create leftist political parties.

To do so, the PT builds from two original points of reference: classism and the extension of full rights of citizenship to all. From its conception of classism comes the party's anti-capitalist outlook, the desire to build a socialist society in accordance with a model constructed by workers and the poor in their own daily struggles. The PT rejects the insurrectional route to power, understood as a frontal attack on state apparatuses that is dissociated from the construction of grassroots organizations. This does not amount to a complete rejection of armed struggle per se, but rather a certain type of armed struggle, which proposes an overthrow of the existing State in order to create a State-led society, and then outlaws independent social movements. The PT's focus on the construction of a powerful civil society –

which pre-dates the crisis of "real socialism" – is based on the party's own experience during the period of military rule and the conservative transition to civilian government.

At the same time, the party's innate anti-capitalist stance led to a critical approach to social-democratic experiments, understood as the social rule of the bourgeois state and a capitalist economy, a system capable of recycling but not resolving the problems inherent in a class-based society. Although a party faction supports social democracy (though even this wing sees the need to "adapt" it to the Third World), their position is a minority one and firmly opposed by the union-led directorate.

Given the rejection of these political options, what possibilities remain for the programmatic and strategic construction of a radical left party?

"The PT understands that, in the transformation of Brazilian society, democracy should be defended and assumed as a strategic value," reads the party's most recent political statement, from May 1990. Putting aside certain reductionist formulas that marked an earlier phase, the PT, says the document, "believes democracy, under-stood as the wide aggregate of citizens' rights to political participation and representation, cannot be seen as a bourgeois value, incorporated with reservations by the workers' movement." The party proposes that "democracy became a universal ideal when it was taken by the working class from the hands of the bourgeoisie, and made a conquest of humanity." The document criticizes the utilitarian vision of "the struggle for democracy" and its use by leftist opposition groups that, once in power, take away rights of collective participation, claiming the workers' reign has arrived.

However, the PT has not abandoned class analysis as central to its project, reiterating that "true democracy is impossible while the bourgeoisie remains the dominant class," and criticizing social demo-crats for subscribing to this illusion. At the same time, so-called experiments in "real socialism" are also attacked for failing to adhere to democratic norms, thereby generating bureaucratic deformations, conformism, accommodation and the stifling of growth and produc-tion. The document says the task of workers' emancipation "demands the radicalization of democracy, against the bourgeoisie, in a socialist world," and concludes: "There will only be true democracy with socialism and no socialism without democracy."

This vague level of programmatic definition, however, has proved insufficient in determining the PT's plan of action in administering municipal governments where it holds power. This problem reached a critical point in 1988, when the party won office in several important cities, including São Paulo. The electoral campaign of incoming mayor Luiza Erundina illustrated the political evolution that integration in the institutional process represented for the PT. Nominated with the support of the party's most radical sectors, Erundina first advocated that the city's regional administrations should exercise "dual-power," an expression of direct democracy.

In the course of the campaign, this issue became secondary; after taking office, Erundina rapidly adopted a more moderate approach toward municipal administration. Her policies were based on the idea of a "public sphere," which she, as the popularly elected mayor, should defend. This orientation was soon tested when strikes by public employees broke out, led by the CUT (and hence the PT). Although São Paulo paid higher salaries than any other municipal government, double-digit monthly inflation during much of Erundina's first year in office led workers to demand salaries that would eat up between 66 and 100 per cent of the city's budget. While recognizing that employees' demands were not without merit, the mayor opposed the strikes and, without using violence, attempted to maintain essential public services throughout their duration. For the first time, the PT was forced to confront the conflict arising from its self-definition as a workers party and the responsibilities stemming from public administration.

The tensions resulting from this conflict are far from resolved, and the party leadership is aware that they will continue to arise each time a PT candidate wins public office and must administer a state constructed by an elite minority in order to dominate and control the dispossessed majority. The PT does not yet have a coherent and fully elaborated strategy for transforming Brazilian capitalism into a democratic socialist society, using the former's own political institutions. The party calls for the most radically democratic form of exercising power allowed by existing structures, but at the same time believes that only by achieving socialism can real democracy be constructed.

The resolution of these questions – or at least the road toward solutions – lies in the future experience of the PT and the mass movements. The administration of municipal governments will create new facts to analyze, and help elaborate answers to questions that must be addressed by a party that seeks to revolutionize Brazilian society after taking power via the ballot box.

7

The 1989 Presidential Campaign

Without fear of being happy . . .
Workers Party slogan for presidential campaign
We proved it's still possible to combine politics with ethics.
Luís Gushiken, PT president, on the 1989 presidential campaign
It's true, only during the last week we were from Woodstock and they came from Chicago to clobber us.
Paulo Delgado, PT federal deputy

With the results of the 1988 municipal elections that brought the PT to power in São Paulo, Porto Alegre, and Vitória, Lula was suddenly considered a serious presidential contender. In the first polls conducted in early 1989, the PT's candidate was running neck and neck with Leonel Brizola with about 12 per cent of the vote while ten other candidates were far behind, none having more than 5 per cent. A December 1988 Gallup poll showed the PT was the country's most popular party, with 25.2 per cent support from respondents.

But Lula's early poll position had as much to do with the disarray of the right and center as it did with the electoral strength of the left. The strategic outlook for the ruling bloc in early 1990 was the worst imaginable. Its largest party, the PMDB, was in an advanced stage of decomposition and disarray. A left-center faction soon abandoned ship to form the new Brazilian Social Democratic Party (PSDB); centrist and rightist sectors were thoroughly demoralized. After twenty-five years of unquestioned rule, the dominant classes found themselves without a party or a candidate for the crucial presidential vote.

Needless to say, that situation was unsettling to a ruling elite that had seen few, if any, risks to its political trajectory. The most important political moments of the century had taken place far from the ballot box: in 1930, Vargas ended the absolute power of the coffee-economy oligarchy and the 1964 coup introduced a process of conservative modernization by means of the military dictatorship.

In the sixty years prior to the 1989 election, just four men had been elected president of the country, and only two had completed their terms in office. The first was General Eurico Dutra, who came to power in 1946 after serving as Minister of War in the deposed Vargas government; the second was Juscelino Kubitschek, whose inauguration was guaranteed by the military, who put down coup plotters. Of the other presidents elected, Getúlio Vargas committed suicide after hearing he had been deposed by the military, and Janio Quadros resigned seven months after taking office. Between 1930 and 1990, then, Brazil had forty-six years without a popularly elected president. Only once, in the case of Kubitschek, did a civilian president complete his term of office and hand over power to an elected president.

Thus the Brazilian political system is not one which tends to legitimize itself via elections. The political and social chaos that led to the 1964 coup represented a crisis in the capacity of the ruling class to rule – a hegemonic crisis in the Gramscian sense. The crisis led the ruling bloc to sever all ties with the popular sectors – an inheritance from Vargas's populism – and put into practice a new phase of capitalist expansion. The maldistribution of income inherent to the new economic model was not compatible with broad alliances beyond a limited elite, which meant the survival of liberal democracy, especially free elections with a universal franchise, was not possible.

During the same period, together with the hegemonic crisis, there also occurred a crisis of the political party system, leading the dominant classes to seek other forms of political "representation." Under these circumstances the armed forces became a sort of military party of the elite. Traditional parties lost force, largely due to systematic repression; in any case the dictatorship had no intention of consulting with Congress about important matters.

The years of military rule did not produce a reconstruction of the bourgeois party system. First, because it wasn't needed; second, because its political proclivities did not permit the consolidation of a party structure with solid mass support. The economic crisis of the civilian-led half of the 1980s and an extremely limited conception of the democratic transition led to the rapid crumbling of the PMDB, leaving the dominant class unprepared to confront the requirement of political legitimation by popular vote.

In 1989, without a solidly based party of its own, the elite was forced to choose among relatively independent candidates able to obtain high popularity ratings. The problem was that there was no candidate acceptable to the ruling class who appeared to have much electoral promise.

Among the early contenders from the center was PMDB Federal Deputy Ulysses Guimarães, speaker of the house. He had been an important opposition leader during the period of military rule, and more recently had led debate when the Constituent Assembly was discussing and writing the 1988 civilian constitution. The PMDB was the largest party in Congress, and its organizational structure in every county in the country automatically made Ulysses a potentially strong contender. But in addition to being the oldest candidate – seventy-three – Guimarães's party was linked to the discredited Sarney administration, which had presided over the worst economic crisis in Brazilian history, a crisis that had progressively worsened during the three years leading up to the election. Inflation seemed to set a new record just about every month it was announced, poverty worsened dramatically, and union groups estimated that real wages plunged by an estimated 25 per cent between 1986 and 1989. In Brazil, though, the rich rarely suffer. Business made huge profits in 1989 – the worst year of the "crisis" – and banks did particularly well. The biggest private financial institution, Bradesco, had a 21.6 per cent return on assets, its best showing since 1985. Business profits overall tripled over 1988 levels as a percentage of assets. Analysts at the Technical Advisory of Capital Markets rightly called it a "golden year."[1]

Another early contender from the center was Mario Covas, leader of the center-left Brazilian Social Democratic Party (PSDB), formed in late 1988 as a breakaway faction of the PMDB. Covas, an ex-mayor of São Paulo, was known for being honest and capable, and had run a reasonably progressive city government. He later received the quiet backing of a number of bishops from the Church's progressive wing, who believed Covas's "capitalism with a human face" was a good option for the country, and one less likely than the PT's program to stir up strong opposition from conservatives and the military.[2] But many leftists did not trust him, especially as he broke with Sarney and the PMDB only in 1988, years after most progressives had long given up hope on the "New Republic." Nor was he trusted by the right, who thought he had been too sympathetic to leftist positions during the constitutional debate.[3]

Conservatives had a number of hopefuls, but they all shared at least one problem: their association with both the military regime and the Sarney government. Among the leading contenders early in the year was Paulo Maluf, the loser in the Electoral College vote of 1984. But Maluf, in addition to being a perennial election loser, had a reputation for dishonesty, arrogance and ultraconservatism that made him unpopular, even with some who detested Lula and Brizola.

Another conservative contender was Aureliano Chaves, ex-vice-president under General Figueiredo, he won the nomination of the Liberal Front Party (PFL), the PMDB's old partner in the "Democratic Alliance," which backed Sarney and was the second largest party in Congress. If his connection to past governments wasn't enough to kill his chances, his absolute lack of charisma was. Portly, balding and dull, Chaves was destined to become one of the campaign's laughingstocks. (In an amusing incident dating from his days as vice-president, Chaves became involved in a feud with his son-in-law, who shot him. He emerged from the hospital in a wheelchair, but, in an attempt to cover up the affair, he said his lack of mobility had been produced by an ingrown toenail.)

Ex-president Janio "Occult Forces" Quadros was seen as the conservatives' best hope early in the year. Quadros, though, with health problems and going blind, did not have the stamina for a long campaign, greatly heightening panic on the right. He formally dropped out of the race in May.

There were a number of other would-be presidents (all told twenty-three candidates took part in the campaign. More than half of them represented minor parties and had no chance at all of winning), but early in the year it looked as if the conservatives might not be able to find anyone to rally behind.

However, the right had long known it would have a marketing problem and, even without a consensus candidate, had general ideas as to what sort of candidate was likely to have a chance at winning the presidency. A key point was to counter the left's call for social change with promises to root out corruption and "moralizing" government. A political project organized by the Federation of Industries of São Paulo State (FIESP), the country's most powerful business lobby, defined the "ideal" candidate as "young," "with administrative experience," "vigorous," and from the political "center." (With this last attribute, image, which can be readily manufactured, is more important than substance. Almost no Brazilian politician who wants to win office at the national level, no matter how reactionary, would ever label him/herself "right-wing," which is tantamount to electoral suicide.)[4]

Fernando Collor de Mello, the governor of the poor northeastern state of Alagoas, was far from perfect but he was as much as conservatives could hope for. Born into one of the country's wealthiest and most powerful families, he entered politics in 1979 when appointed by the military regime as mayor of the northeastern city of Maceió. Three years later, he was elected to Congress on the ticket of the Social Democratic Party, the official party of the dictatorship. When millions of Brazilians took to the streets in 1984 to demand free presidential elections, Collor surprised his colleagues by backing the amendment for direct elections that had been offered by PMDB Deputy Dante de Oliveira. When the amendment lost, though, Collor cast his Electoral College vote for Maluf (who was also the best man at his marriage in 1984 to Rosanne Malta, whose family is one of the most prominent in Maceió).

In 1986, with Sarney's popularity soaring as a result of the temporarily successful Cruzado Plan, Collor joined the ruling PMDB, in the sort of opportunistic move Brazilian politicians have raised to an art form. He first came to national attention the same year, when, after being elected governor of Alagoas state, he refused to pay the exorbitant salaries of an elite group of civil servants known as "maharajas." Many of these maharajas earned up to $10,000 a month for government jobs they rarely showed up for. Collor also began attacking Sarney after the economy deteriorated and the president's approval rating entered a freefall.

When it became clear the PMDB would not nominate him as its presidential candidate, Collor switched parties again, forming the brand new National Reconstruction Party (PRN) to launch his own bid. He was considered to have almost no chance of winning, but, with a vacuum created by public disgust with the country's largest parties and most prominent politicians, Collor became the media's darling and a political "phenomenon." Calling himself the "hunter of maharajas," Collor ran as an outsider and claimed to be independent of traditional politicians and the economic elite. He also backed a negotiated settlement with the banks on the debt issue, in contrast to the left's call for a moratorium, increased foreign investment, privatization of state firms and lowering the state deficit via spending cuts and fiscal reform. But these latter proposals took a back-seat to the anti-corruption theme, and Collor, despite his conservative economic recipe, portrayed himself as a modern European-style social democrat and railed against Brazil's "jungle capitalism."

A charismatic populist, Collor developed a big following among the rural poor. During campaign speeches, he promised to attend to the needs of the "shirtless and shoeless," who have been left behind by the development process. Never mentioned at all, naturally, were his connections with the military regime that had taken the clothes off their backs. By April 1989 he had a huge lead in the polls over Lula and Brizola, at which point many conservatives, who initially were divided among a number of right-of-center candidates, scrambled to join his bandwagon.

Key to Collor's early surge, particularly in helping promote his preposterously absurd image as a mortal foe of the establishment, was the backing of media magnate Roberto Marinho, owner of the powerful TV Globo network and the Rio daily paper, *O Globo*. The network, fourth largest in the world after the three American giants, produces hugely popular soap operas (movie star Sonia Braga got her start in one) which has helped give it an estimated 70 per cent audience share and tremendous power to influence politics.

Marinho obtained a concession for TV Globo from the military shortly after the coup and he strongly backed the regime while his network expanded throughout the country. When *Jornal Nacional*, Globo's prime-time nightly news program, celebrated its twenty-fifth anniversary in 1989, a joke making the rounds in Rio was that the program should be listed in the Guinness Book of World Records for "Longest Streak of Non-criticism for Government by News Show." One example of how Marinho's network earned this reputation came in January 1984, when 300,000 Brazilians in São Paulo took part in a "Direct Elections Now!" rally. *Jornal Nacional* showed film footage but informed viewers the crowd was part of celebrations commemorating the city's anniversary. The network has since become far more sophisticated and, with a large percentage of the population either illiterate or semi-literate – and extremely vulnerable to media manipulation – Marinho is rightly considered one of the country's most powerful men.[5]

But then the generals, who foresaw a trend towards urbanization when they took charge – an ominous trend, from their point of view, in terms of social control – always looked upon the network as a future pillar of support for the establishment. In 1960, the year of the last presidential election prior to the 1989 vote, the franchise was limited to 25 per cent of the electorate. Also a majority of the population lived in the interior where their votes were easily controlled by the landed oligarchy. In 1989, only a quarter of the population lived in the interior and 55 per cent voted in December's balloting. TV Globo currently plays the part – which it began to play during the dictatorship – that money and clientelism did thirty years ago.

Marinho is not shy about pushing his weight around. In 1987, he told a *New York Times* reporter, "Yes, I use [power], but I always do so patriotically, trying to correct things, looking for the best paths for the country and its states." He admitted he had worked to defeat Brizola's hand-picked successor, anthropologist Darcy Ribeiro, in the 1986 gubernatorial election in Rio de Janeiro state.(Marinho's candidate was the victorious Wellington Moreira Franco, a self-professed Maoist in his youth, who then joined the military-backed PDS to run for governor in 1982. For his 1986 bid, he switched to the PMDB.) "At a determined moment, I became convinced that Mr Leonel Brizola was a bad governor. He transformed the marvelous city that is Rio into a place of beggars and peddlers. . . . I really used all possibilities to defeat him in the election," Marinho said. (He failed to mention the fact that in the 1982 election Globo showed early returns with Franco far ahead, in an apparent attempt to help an independent counting agency cheat Brizola of victory. The fraud was uncovered, and denounced, by the *Jornal do Brasil* radio station, which effectively put an end to the scheme.) Finally, in explaining why TV Globo almost completely ignored a 1987 general strike called by a broad segment of the union movement, Marinho said, "It was not good for Brazil."[6]

Marinho was an early admirer of Collor and in late 1987 TV Globo sent to Alagoas a reporter whose primary task was to report on the good deeds of the then governor. When he took off in the polls, Marinho tossed all his chips into Collor's basket. The tycoon was so confident of victory by June, when Collor had 45 per cent poll support while the other candidate split the rest, that Globo threw a celebration party at the Rio discotheque "Hippopotamus." Many observers at the time said Collor would win a majority in the November vote and a second round would not even be necessary.

Despite his huge lead, Collor had a big Achilles' heel – his past. In addition to his support for the dictatorship, there was plenty of information indicating he had run shady administrations when mayor of Maceió and governor of Alagoas. A few newspapers published well-documented charges – completely ignored by Marinho's properties, as well as the other networks – which included:

– He gave a $400,000 state contract to a firm owned by his chief economic advisor, Zelia Cardoso de Mello – no relation – without competitive bidding.

– He appointed thousands to high-paying state jobs – creating the same "maharajas" he claimed to be a foe of – just before resigning to run for president. In 1982, when mayor of Maceió, he appointed 3,000 public employees in his final week in office alone.

– He spent almost $1 million on official propaganda extoling his administration's work during his last five months as governor. Over half the money went to media outlets owned by his family.

– In 1987, a state bank exchanged a debt of $124,000 with the family-owned business TV Gazeta for free ads on the station as well as on three radio stations and a newspaper owned by his family. The signee of the deal for the bank was a man who was one of Collor's principal supporters during his gubernatorial run. The deal led to the bankruptcy of the state bank.

– He spent more than $1 million in state money intended for emergency expenditures – over 5,000 per cent more than budgeted – between January and May of 1989. Some of this money was used to buy gifts of flowers, crystal and silverware for friends and political allies. The *Folha de São Paulo* newspaper estimated that these funds could have paid for 200 low-cost houses for the poor or paid the entire year's salaries for employees at a state agency charged with caring for abandoned children.

– Collor, the self-proclaimed foe of the rich elite, had vowed during his campaign for governor that he would take on the state's sugar barons. Instead, after a court ruled that a tax imposed on the sugar-owners was illegal, Collor signed a deal reimbursing to them $100 million, a figure another court later ruled to be twice as large as it should have been. Collor also built a number of roads that serviced the sugar plantations and failed to appropriate a fraction of the baron's lands, as he had promised, to carry out an agrarian reform program.

And despite his claim to be a crusading reformer, Collor's hastily formed PRN had a decidedly rightist tilt. A majority of the twenty-three deputies who joined the party had voted to give Sarney –

Collor's arch-enemy on the campaign trail – a five year term, and also voted against the left's agrarian reform plank during constitutional debate in 1988, a proposal which was ultimately defeated by a small margin. The only leftist among the twenty-three was Renan Calheiros from Collor's home state of Alagoas. When Collor was mayor of Maceió, Calheiros, then a member of the state assembly for the opposition MDB, called him a "prince of corruption."

Some of the elected officials that joined the PRN, which was supposedly going to build a "New Brazil," were:

– Geovani Borges of northern Amapá state, who voted for Maluf in the 1984 Electoral College vote, and was listed as a "traitor of the people" by the Pastoral Land Commission because of his opposition to land reform.

– José Gomes of the central state of Goiás, best known for organizing demonstrations in favour of permanent residence for former Paraguayan dictator Alfredo Stroessner, who sought exile in Brazil after being toppled in early 1989.

– João Castelo, from the northern state of Maranhão. He became a fierce critic of Sarney in recent years, but the two had been political cronies for years, dating back to their membership in ARENA. Sarney intervened in his favour in 1978 and Castelo was named governor of the state by the military. Collor, in what can only be considered exaggeration bordering on delusion, called him the "symbol of resistance to the New Republic," when Castelo joined his campaign.

– Mario de Oliveira, from Minas Gerais, who received a piece of federally owned land in the center of Belo Horizonte for having voted in favor of a five-year presidential term.

– Arnaldo Faria de Sá, from São Paulo, who ran as vice-mayor on Maluf's ticket in 1988.

– José Carlos Martinez, from the wealthy southern state of Parana. His family was accused of having illegally obtained land in the state by forcing out peasant families. Martinez himself was a UDR sympathizer and owns four television stations, one of them obtained from Sarney.[7]

Until mid-September, this information was available only to readers of the few big city newspapers that ran the charges, who make up a very small percentage of the population. (The country's two best newspapers – there is no alternative left press – *Folha de São Paulo* and the Rio-based *Jornal do Brasil*, have combined readership of slightly more than 300,000, in a country of 150 million. The two other major dailies, O *Globo* and O *Estado de São Paulo* – the latter almost as conservative and partial as the former – have a total readership of about 400,000. Neither published a fraction of the information available about Collor's past activities.) On September 15, though, all political parties began to receive free television time, based on their representation in Congress, for a period of two months. When the charges of corruption and Collor's close ties to the military were aired, the favorite began to drop in the polls. His popularity fell especially rapidly among the better educated and residents of major urban centers.

But Collor's core supporters, the uneducated, unorganized, rural lower class, mostly remained in his corner. Helio Jaguaribe, one of the country's leading sociologists, says the Brazilian poor can be divided into three broad categories. First, there is a largely urban sector that is involved in unions, the Christian Base Communities, neighborhood organizations and other popular movements. This group tends to be class-conscious and supportive of the PT. Second are those who have migrated from the interior to urban centers but are largely unorganized. They tend to support charismatic, populist candidates, such as Brizola, based on personal rather than political criteria. Third are the unorganized rural poor, who are the most impoverished. This sector tends to have a "moralistic" view of the world, believing unethical, dishonest politicians, not economic and political structures, are at the root of their problems (and their votes are often controlled by the large landowners). Collor, who ranted and railed against corruption, was seen as a "Salvador da Patria" by many of these people and most never abandoned him.

Meanwhile, as Collor ran ahead in the polls, Lula had been struggling. A wave of strikes in March and April by unions tied to the CUT – and misrepresented by the PT's opponents – were detrimental to the campaign, as they created a tremendous media backlash, scared the middle class, and some sectors of the poor (while helping Lula with labor movement leaders, as he was the only major candidate to back the strikers). The stoppages began with a two-day general strike called by the CUT and the CGT for March 14 and 15. The strike shut down twelve state capitals and was felt strongly in every part of the country; it was certainly the most successful of the eleven general strikes called during Brazil's history, being joined by close to half of the economically active population. (PT mayors supported the strikers. Luiza Erundina in São Paulo ordered the state bus company, which owns about one-third of the city's buses, to keep its vehicles off the streets. On the other hand, she had city workers who didn't show up at the office docked a day's pay. In Porto Alegre, ex-bank union leader Olivio Dutra picketed with strikers before heading to the office. And in Vitória, Mayor Vitor Buaiz joined strikers in a downtown march, and was briefly involved in a scuffle with a state trooper.)

But by late April, major strikes were rampant, and included in the final week of that month alone, a nationwide stoppage of bank workers, a strike at nearly all of the country's major ports by dockworkers; stoppages by metalworkers in São Paulo, Rio de Janeiro, and Minas Gerais states, and strikes by schoolteachers in eleven states. All told, nearly two million workers were off the job.

Violence during the strikes, or tied to past labor disputes, created the impression that the country was on the edge of chaos. In one example, and one very detrimental to Lula's bid, a PT militant, Antonio Ferreira, on April 25, tried to put a homemade bomb into a branch of a Bradesco bank agency in the northeastern city of Recife during the bankworkers' strike. (He was acting alone, and the action was later condemned by the PT.) About a week later, on May 2, a monument designed by architect Oscar Niemeyer and dedicated to the three striking workers killed by the army in 1988, was blown up in Volta Redonda with forty pounds of plastic explosives – on the day after it was inaugurated. The blast blew out windows in buildings almost 1,000 feet from the monument, and was heard a mile and a half away. (Right-wing terrorists were the key suspects, though then Justice Minister Oscar Dias Correa speculated that the left might be behind the blast, in a clever ploy to discredit the government.) Soon after, striking metalworkers clashed with police as they marched in São Bernardo do Campo. Five workers suffered gunshot wounds when troopers opened fire, and seventeen soldiers were injured by stones.[8]

The major media's coverage (and government propaganda efforts, discussed shortly) did not discuss in great detail some revealing aspects behind the strikes – namely, that workers' real wages had been so drastically reduced during the previous years that they were desperate. Labor conflicts had grown more and more frequent after the return of civilian rule, as pent-up demands for better wages exploded. But they really took off in 1986 (83 strikes took place in 1980, 420 in 1984, 2,282 during 1986, the first year of civilian rule, 2,313 in 1987, and 2,241 in 1988; during the first four months of 1989, there were 1,297).[9] The final straw for workers came in January 1989, when the Sarney government launched its third major anti-inflation plan in three years (new national currencies were created as part of two of them), which slashed pay. The average real wage in São Paulo industry fell from the equivalent of about $233 in December 1988, to $193 in February 1989, with the same trend registered throughout the country. Meanwhile, the number of strikes soared from 220 in February to 479 in March and about the same number in April.[10]

The military launched a fierce attack, portraying the strikers as rabble-rousing ne'er-do-wells, who cared nothing about the "little guy." The generals produced a document containing an odd mix of Marxist rhetoric and classic fascism at the time which said, "Unpatriotic are those who trick the working class, utilizing the sacred social right – the strike [which they had virtually outlawed for twenty-five years] – to intimidate society and disrupt the means of production, almost always against the will of the workers, who desire to keep their organizations functioning."

The government also took a heavy-handed approach. First, Sarney decreed a bill which; (1) made a strike legal only if it had not only majority support at a union assembly, but also the approval of more than one-third of all union members. As one magazine noted, "It is a quorum that is almost impossible to obtain";[11] (2) provided for stiff penalties for violence on the picket line, and prevented sympathizers from other unions from participating in strike activities; and (3) stipulated that in "essential sectors" – broadly defined to include electricity, transport, hospitals, water, certain banking services, and eight other categories – strikes could only be declared with forty-eight-hour notice. Decio Guimarães, a Rio-based labor lawyer with the CUT, said "The only workers not considered to be in essential services are samba dancers." (Mario Amato of FIESP criticized the new strike law, and said the government was trying to impose a "regime of terror." CUT president Jair Meneguelli promised unions would ignore it. But only the latter was called into federal police headquarters to explain his comments. Sarney's bill was later modified by Congress but many of the restrictive measures passed largely intact).

The government also resorted to the old standby of dirty tricks to discredit the labor movement. Federal police presented a pamphlet, which they claimed was produced by the CUT, that instructed strike leaders on the usefulness of stoning their opponents during labor disputes. CUT leaders denounced the pamphlet as a fake, and its style, similar to fraudulent documents created by the generals during the dictatorship, supported the federation's claim. In a final display of the government's fondness of tactics used by the dictatorship, Justice Minister Correa offered state governors federal troops to take on the strikers. (One magazine reported that the government's tough line had been induced by military officials. Ivan de Souza Mendes, the head of the National Information Service, reportedly met with three cabinet ministers, and said, "The hour has arrived to put an end to the strikes that are immobilizing the country.")[12]

Also hurting the campaign were charges by the PT's opponents that the cities administered by PT mayors were mismanaged and chaotic. The media gave tremendous play to the charges, to the extent that it sometimes seemed the residents of those cities made up the entire population (The PT expelled five of the thirty-six mayors elected on the party's ticket in the 1989 elections, accusing them of betraying principles after winning office. "The party does not accept that mayors change shirts after the elections," Secretary-General José Dirceu said of those expelled.[13] But those disowned were from small rural towns with a combined population of less than a few hundred thousand. Some 23 million people still lived in cities administered by the PT after they were expelled.)

Most of the attention focused on Mayor Luiza Erundina of São Paulo, partly because of the city's size and prominence and partly due to Brazil's endemic sexism. Erundina did not run a flawless administration – which could hardly be expected as she was in her first year in office – and her approval rating during 1990 was among the lowest of all the mayors who had been elected the previous year.[14] She had major problems with the media, and was also involved in several well-publicized disputes with the São Paulo PT (the party has a history of fighting with its own elected officials), which did not approve of some of her appointees or activities. City residents also complained that she had failed to improve the rickety system of public transportation, and that refuse collection was worse than under the previous mayor, none other than ex-president Janio Quadros.

Bur Erundina had a number of problems not of her own making (not the least of which was the huge expectations the population had of a PT administration, plus the fact that the party had a minority position in the City Council and the mayor was unable to gain approval for many of her plans). For starters, the federal and state governments withheld funds for health, housing, and sanitation projects that City Hall was legally entitled to. The federally owned Caixa

Economica Federal simply refused to allocate funds for low-cost housing projects and the Sarney government failed to free money set for health projects, money which was required to be turned over under the 1988 constitution.[15] Erundina also inherited a huge debt from Quadros, who had begun a number of megaprojects that had to be abandoned due to lack of funds and/or usefulness. (Quadros was an eccentric showman. One of his acts in office was to put double-decker red buses on the streets, as he considered London to be a model city.)

The mayor and the party rarely received credit for their good deeds. For example, PT leaders tried to change the way politicians tradition-ally did business, which generally meant payoffs, sinecures for cronies, and many other varieties of crass corruption. City Council President Eduardo Suplicy launched investigations into past shenani-gans by local representatives that resulted in eleven former officials being charged with corruption – including four past presidents of the Council (a very suspicious fire that started late one night in a Council room filled with old legal documents destroyed some papers, and slowed investigations). Suplicy's actions did receive media attention, but no one dubbed the PT the "anti-corruption party" or promoted Suplicy – much less Lula – as "the hunter of maharajas."[16]

In one of the few positive articles on the PT's mayors during their first months in office, the liberal magazine *Isto É/Senhor* noted: "There were 36 mayors – today there are 31. But among the more than 3,000 that exist . . . they are the ones that lead the national championship of centimeters of news in conservative newspapers." The magazine gave a largely positive assessment of the party's officeholders, saying, "The PT . . . arrived in power speaking of changes, [and] changed little. But what changed, changed for the better." Among the improve-ments were an unprecedented "zero rate of corruption," and an attempt to increase democracy at the local level, which would amount to a true revolution in centralized, bureaucratized Brazil: "In Campi-nas, assemblies proliferate in which Mayor Jaco Bittar discusses priorities with the people. In São Paulo, residents' associations debate the next budget. In Porto Alegre, the administrative reform brought together all interested parties for discussions, including the employees' union, affiliated to the CGT, the PT's rival. In Santos, the PT even ended the practice of electric shock treatment at the Santa Isabel psychiatric hospital, and transformed what was an inferno of badly treated patients into a model clinic."[17]

The commotion over the strikes and the PT's mayors seriously weakened Lula's campaign, which hit rock-bottom in July when he had only 6 per cent support in one public opinion survey. He remained bogged down in the polls until October, along with Mario Covas of the PSDB, right-of-center Guilherme Afif Domingos of the Liberal Party, who briefly seemed to have a shot at breaking out of the pack to challenge Collor on the right, and Paulo Maluf. All four fluctuated in the polls between around 4 and 8 per cent. In second place, but far behind Collor, was Brizola of the Democratic Labor Party (PDT).

Brizola is a mythical figure to many and has a fanatical following in the states of Rio de Janeiro and Rio Grande do Sul, where he is an ex-governor. He was chief executive of the latter in 1964, and was one of only two that sent out state militias to oppose the coup. After spending fifteen years in exile, he returned to Brazil in 1979 when the amnesty was decreed.

Brizola has a reputation for opportunism, however, and made alliances with conservative sectors to try to increase his share of the rural vote. (For this reason he is not trusted by many members of the PT. Several years ago, Lula said Brizola would "step on his own mother's neck to get elected president.") While not given much of a chance of finishing first in the November vote, most observers thought Brizola was sure to come second and win a place in the runoff.

But while the PDT candidate failed to gain any significant support, hovering for months at between 12 and 15 per cent poll support, the PT's campaign began picking up steam. The campaign's momentum was first registered on the streets during September, and was only picked up by the polls a month later. Lula had been conducting an exhausting campaign schedule for months, often holding as many as seven events per day. And attendance at rallies was soaring. On September 17, Lula drew 50,000 flag-waving, wildly enthusiastic supporters to the Praça da Sé in São Paulo, a crowd record at that time. He continued to attract large numbers in the days ahead and at the next major rally, held on October 18, 60,000 supporters jammed the center of Belo Horizonte to hear the PT candidate. In November, as the vote neared, the crowds grew enormously, culminating with two huge rallies in Rio and São Paulo, held less than a week before the vote, and which attracted 200,000 and 250,000 people, respectively. By then, poll support had grown as well, and Lula and Brizola went into the final stretch in a virtual dead heat.

What caused the turnaround? In a post-campaign analysis, Lula's chief press aide Ricardo Kotscho wrote that a key reason was simply the free TV and radio time that began on September 15. Whereas prior to that date, the PT had received much negative media coverage, a bigger problem was that Lula's candidacy was simply ignored (except by *Folha de São Paulo*, the country's most liberal newspaper: while the paper is certainly not pro–PT – a reputation it has in some circles – it is the only news organ in the country that gives major space to the left). As Kotscho said: "The information blockade was broken the moment that the free political propaganda time began on radio and TV, revealing for many incredulous people what was in fact happening with the PT's campaign. Columnists were obliged to remember that Lula's campaign existed, and even the major media could no longer deny or omit one fact: since the Direct Elections Now! campaign in 1984, Brazil had seen nothing like it."[18]

Another key factor in Lula's surge, particularly in the northeast, was the work of Church activists. Traditionally, voting in the region was controlled by large landowners, the so-called *coronels*, who long dominated the region and continue to exercise significant influence. The *coronels* provided food, transport, and money on election day – and added treats afterwards if votes corresponded to their expectations. (Often, peasants would receive half of a currency note or one of a pair of boots. They received the other half after the vote if the *coronels* felt they hadn't been doublecrossed.) Church and peasant activists worked hard to counter the efforts of the region's powers-that-be. One priest in the Casa Amarela neighborhood of Recife was especially bold. Reginaldo Veloso put up a billboard in front of his church which said "Think before you vote. Are you a boss or a worker? Of the candidates for president, who is a boss and who is a worker? Will you vote for the boss?"[19] Other priests even put Lula's campaign literature next to the saints on church altars.

As Lula began to pick up steam, many Brazilian businessmen panicked. FIESP head Mario Amato warned shortly before the first-round vote, "If Lula wins, there will be chaos in the country." He predicted "800,000 businessmen will flee the country" in the event of a PT win. (Amato was scheduled to leave the country for a brief trip to Europe, and PT leaders publicly joked that they hoped he would postpone the trip, as he was the party's top vote-getter.) Coffee-grower Ricardo Ticault said "Lula as president would be the end of the world." Others even began to look upon Brizola in a new light. Supermarket magnate João Carlos Paes Mendonça said, "We could deal with Brizola because he defends capitalism and free enterprise. Lula doesn't."

Roberto Marinho was also unhappy, and did everything possible to keep Lula out of the runoff (though for a time conservatives, and Collor, thought Lula might be an easier candidate to beat than Brizola, as they said the PT was too sectarian to attract substantial support). Two weeks before the first-round vote ultraright presidential candidate Ronaldo Caiado (then president of the Rural Democratic Union, who "peaked" at about 1.5 per cent support),[20] charged during a televised debate that an illegal contribution to Lula's campaign had been shuttled through the office of Luiza Erundina in São Paulo. Though there was no proof of any wrongdoing – and a subsequent investigation showed there was none – the media, led by Globo, trumpeted the charges (calling it the "Lubeca case," after the company involved) up until the day of the vote, and it definitely slowed the campaign's momentum. As Lula charged, "They are trying to steal the PT's political virginity."

On November 15, Brazil went to the polls for the first time since 1960. Lula, himself voting for president for the first time in his life, kissed his ballot and deposited it in an urn at a polling station near his home in São Bernardo do Campo. Then the wait began. Vote-counting takes time in Brazil especially as some ballot boxes in rural regions have to be transported to vote-counting centers by boat and horseback. (In one incident reported in the press, a jaguar attacked a horse-riding election official as he was delivering ballots to a regional election center.) Also, TV networks do not make iron-clad projections seconds after the polls close. But when the counting was complete some four days later, Collor had 28 per cent while Lula, with 16.5 per cent, just squeaked past Brizola with 16 per cent, a difference of less than 450,000 votes out of a total of about 72 million cast.

Lula's margin of victory was probably provided by the hard work of the PT's estimated one million nationwide activists, a network that no other party could rely on. (Thanks mostly to these militants, the PT is known as the "party of arrival" because its candidates always finish strong.) The work of rural activists was absolutely crucial. Lula finished second throughout most of the north and northeast, and made especially impressive showings in Pernambuco (30 per cent, just behind Collor), 21 per cent in Rio Grande do Norte (eight points behind Collor), Bahia (22 per cent, seven points, behind Collor) and Paraíba (21.4 per cent, ten points behind Collor). In the state of

Tocantins Lula finished a poor third, with only 9 per cent support. But in the Parrot's Beak region, Lula ran strong, obtaining one-quarter of the votes cast. "What the PT was able to get here was because of Padre Josimo,"said state party secretary, Manoel Panelada.

Lula also did well in Xapuri, the small Amazonian village in the state of Acre where rubber-tapper and union leader Chico Mendes – a PT militant – worked until he was assassinated in December 1988. Lula received 1,903 votes in Xapuri, almost one-third of the total, and took first place with a more than 600-vote advantage over Collor. Far back in third place was Ulysses Guimarães, with 440 votes. The PT's strong showing – despite a vigorous Collor push in the area – was due largely to the work of Mendes's colleagues in the local union. After the vote, Jorge Gomes Pinheiro, who replaced Mendes as union president after his murder, said, "We aren't a party-affiliated entity. But we're sure the huge majority of our 2,000 members are campaigning for Lula." And Mendes's widow, Ilzamar Gadelha Mendes, said, "Lula's name hasn't stopped growing since the start of the campaign and now we're working so that he wins the state [in the second round]."[21]

Many rubber-tappers in other regions voted for Lula as well. *Jornal do Brasil* told the story of Elizeu Rodrigues de Almeida, a tapper who lived in São Pedro do Ico, near the Bolivian border, who left his home ten days beforehand so he could reach the Acre state capital of Rio Branco to cast his vote for Lula. Elizeu walked for two days through the forest until he reached the Iaco river, then hitched a ride on a boat that six days later left him in the village of Sena Madureira. From there, he hitched another ride on the back of a truck for the two-day ride to Rio Branco. When asked whether the trip was worth the trouble, he said, "Ah, it was worth it, yes," and explained that he had made a promise to vote for "the candidate who was Chico Mendes's friend." After casting his ballot, Elizeu paid the equivalent of about one dollar to send a message to his wife on a local radio station's "Message Hour," It read: "Attention Dona Jardelina, in São Pedro do Ico, on the Iaco river. Elizeu advises that he had a good trip. I already voted and tomorrow I'll be returning. Bless the children."[22]

Though total first-round votes were roughly split between leftist and conservative candidates, few gave Lula a chance at a December runoff victory. The media and conservatives confidently predicted he was far too radical to win an electoral majority. First polls, which gave Collor a lead of up to fifteen points, seemed to indicate the optimism of the right was well founded. Making matters worse, the PT was short on funds. Lula had travelled to campaign appearances on commercial flights until a few weeks before the first-round vote, while businessmen quietly poured money into Collor's war chest. As a result, the conservative candidate had fourteen planes at his disposal and eighty private security guards accompanied him around the country. (The PT's campaign funds were largely raised by contributions at factory gates, at rallies, and by selling T-shirts and other campaign paraphernalia. The party received a tremendous piece of luck during the first round, when Vladimir Palmeira, a federal deputy from Rio de Janeiro state, won a $1 million lottery in late August and donated $100,000 to Lula's campaign – a sum almost half as much as had been raised up to that point.)

Collor immediately went on the attack. He accused the party of wanting to take power by force, said a Lula victory would result "in a bloodbath," and predicted a crushing victory. Collor's campaign also showed it was adept in the use of dirty tricks, distributing to the press a pamphlet which staffers said was produced by a PT youth group. The pamphlet said if the party didn't win the December runoff, the PT should take power by force "even if [it required] the spilling of blood." Collor's workers also dug up a speech by PT Federal Deputy Florestan Fernandes that praised Chinese dictator Deng Xiaoping shortly after the brutal crackdown in 1989 on demonstrators in Peking's Square of Celestial Peace, and distributed a small part of a 1985 interview in which Lula said democracy "makes direct elections unnecessary."

As it turned out, the pamphlet was a fake, and the Lula interview was taken out of context. His point was that "democracy" involves not merely voting but also popular control over the government. In the same interview Lula had called for free elections in the Soviet Union and Cuba. Finally, Fernandes had indeed praised Deng but his was a lonely voice in the PT; the party broke relations with the Chinese Communist Party shortly after the massacre.[23]

Another tactic employed by Collor, and hyped by the media, was to stress the PT's losses in the first round in many of the cities it administered, most notably São Paulo. PRN campaign ads said that these proved the party was "incomPTent." But as Lula pointed out, many candidates had lost in cities where their party occupied City Hall. For example, Mario Covas, who finished fourth in the first round with around 10 per cent of the vote, lost in Manaus and Belo

Horizonte, two important state capitals the PSDB controlled. Collor was helped by the fact that the PRN was a new party and had few officeholders. But in many major cities where the mayor backed Collor, Lula won, such as Osasco, São Paulo, and Recife, Pernambuco. The PT also ran strong in the industrial suburbs of São Paulo, picking up around 35 per cent of the vote, and won in all three cities where they controlled the mayor's office.

Despite the long odds, Lula ran a strong campaign. In place of Collor's vague promises of a moral clean-up, he had clear proposals to revamp the economy and democratize Brazilian society. But the PT, recognizing the difficulty of immediately implementing all of its projects, did not call for "socialism now," but instead, at least in the short term, a "redistributive shock within capitalism." The party's key planks were:

1. An immediate suspension of interest payments on the foreign debt, which make internal investments and social spending impossible. During Sarney's five-year term, the country paid out $56 billion to creditors and received only $16 billion in new loans from banks and international lenders. Private banks, which had heaped money on the generals, received about $32 billion in interest payments during this period, while lending only about $5 billion – a net gain of $27 billion in only five years.[24]

The PT said a good part of the country's debt resulted from an increase in international interest rates after 1979 – Brazilian loans had "floating interest" clauses – and was not legitimate. Lula promised an audit and repudiation of part of the debt, estimated to be 40 per cent, and repayment, at less burdensome terms, on the rest.

2. A "democratization," but not privatization, of Brazil's large state sector. PT economic advisor Aloísio Mercadante said in a newspaper interview, "We're against the idea, defended even by some progressives, of a minimum state sector. We are also against the idea that a smaller state means less poverty. We think the state is necessary to propel development. The fundamental problem of the [Brazilian] state is that it is controlled by business groups that appropriate public resources for their own interests."[25]

And if ever Marx's dictum that "the state is the executive committee of the bourgeoisie" had real meaning, it is in Brazil. In addition to "creating a favorable investment climate," the military, and Sarney, heaped favors on domestic and multinational business interests. In

1988, there were twenty-eight types of fiscal incentive that benefited everyone from export firms to mining companies, and which totaled around $5.5 billion annually. Another $2.2 billion per year were laid out in direct subsidies, all to private enterprise. Subsidies to cattle-ranchers alone were estimated at several billion dollars during the last twenty years, with much of this money directly or indirectly being used to destroy the Amazon. (Though preservation of the rainforest is a hot international topic, environmental issues were almost completely unaddressed in the election campaign. Both Lula and Collor said they would protect the Amazon but rejected any schemes that threatened Brazilian "sovereignty," such as debt-for-nature swaps.) Government favors, often doled out on the basis of connections to powerbrokers, helped create an economy dominated by cartels and oligopolies. The top fifty business groups – excluding banks – accounted for an incredible 38.3 per cent of sales in 1989.[26]

At the same time, the PT did not propose adding to the state sector and supported some private enterprise, particularly in agriculture. "The experience of 'actually existing socialism' in the entire world demonstrates that total state control and centralized planning don't lead to the development of productive forces or an elevation of the quality of life," wrote party economic analyst Paul Singer. (He says his ideas have been greatly influenced by the book *The Politics of Feasible Socialism*, by University of Glasgow professor Alec Nove, who foresees a key role for the market in socialist societies.)

Deputy Sampaio laid out the party's vision of the role of the state;

The state . . . has a strategic importance . . . [in the promotion] of nascent industries, such as computers and biotechnology, among others. On top of this, the country's economic development continues to require the presence of the state to the extent that it opens fronts of economic expansion, defining schemes of financing investments, building up infrastructure, and refereeing the competition between national and foreign capital. The role of the state . . . finally, is to guarantee education, health, housing and transport, to overcome the social apartheid in which authoritarianism has placed us."[27]

3. An all-out attack on inflation. Perhaps surprisingly, the PT rejected a wage and price freeze, and recommended sectoral negotiations between labor and business to bring prices down. Freezes have been largely discredited in Brazil, rightly or wrongly, as they were the

basis of three failed economic emergency plans by the Sarney government.

The PT, of course, rejected the orthodox, IMF plan to control inflation via decreased state spending to balance the public deficit. Singer says the Fund approach is particularly absurd in Brazil, where the public deficit is estimated to be around 4–6 per cent – not significantly different from the US average during the Reagan years, when inflation dropped sharply.[28]

And Lula, saying the war on inflation could not be won on the backs of the poor, promised to double the minimum wage in his first year in office and bring it up to the equivalent of $253 per month in 1994 – its real value in 1940. (It was worth only about $75 per month in 1989. Lula said doubling the minimum wage was "easy, because it's moving from nothing to nothing.")[29] These sorts of wages, of course, are the root of the social inequality that exists in the country, which, incredibly, worsened during the five-year civilian administration of Sarney. Statistics for 1989 published by the World Bank also showed Brazil among the worst countries in the world in terms of social inequality. While the top 20 per cent of the population received 66.6 per cent of the national income, the bottom 60 per cent took home only 16.4 per cent. Comparable figures for India, not exactly a model of social justice, were 49.4 and 30.1 per cent. In First World Belgium, the figures are 36 and 40.2 per cent.

The PT also proposed increased state spending for housing, education healthcare, and other social programs, while redirecting investments to meet basic needs. Economic advisor Mercadante said during the campaign, "The problem of Brazil today is not to produce sophisticated automobiles. Our true challenge is to end the lines at bus stops."

4. A large-scale agrarian reform to benefit Brazil's 12 million landless peasants. The PT pledged to appropriate all properties of over 1,500 hectares (the ceiling was to have been as low as 500 hectares in some regions) and redistribute them to poor farmers.

5. Strict curbs on the military, which continues to exercise tremendous power. During Sarney's term in office, the generals helped block the agrarian reform program, played a major role in determining environmental policy, especially for the Amazon, pressured Congress to retain a constitutional clause allowing them to "maintain internal order," and sent troops out on several occasions to break up strikes. Army Minister Pires often seemed content to make policy pronounce-

ments, and to act, without bothering to consult with Sarney, osten-
sibly the commander-in-chief of the armed forces. Alfred Stepan,
dean of the school of international affairs at Columbia University, said
that of forty democracies in the world he had surveyed, nowhere did
the armed forces have as many prerogatives as they did in Brazil. He
told *Jornal do Brasil* in a November 19, 1989 interview, "Brazil became
a democratic regime in 1985 with a high level of military participation
[and] . . . the situation hasn't changed. That signifies the consolidation
of prerogatives, not of democracy." Lula pledged to create a unified
Defense Ministry, which would reduce the armed forces to one
cabinet position, and said he would extinguish the National Information Service.[30] Not surprisingly, military officials discreetly backed
Collor's campaign (although he had not been their first choice in most
cases: many military officials didn't trust Collor's apparent lack of
emotional self-control). Though the generals denied they would stage
a coup if Lula won the election, Sarney reportedly told friends he
feared the possibility, as did many others.

   6. Though foreign policy was not a major feature of the campaign,
the PT proposed a distancing of relations with the USA. According to
Deputy Sampaio, "To deny the imperialist policies of the United
States at various historical moments is to deny an established reality
. . . they are one country and we are another. Our economy is
massively dependent on theirs and that can't continue. [A PT govern-
ment] will be more independent, will not be subservient, and will have
relations of independence."[31]

Lula moderated his discourse during the second round in an attempt to
broaden the PT's appeal to the middle class and attract support from
more moderate parties, especially the PSDB.[32] But PT leaders never
hid the radical nature of the party's program, and stressed that a
socialist society was their goal. "We have to calm the citizenry. We're
not going to take anybody's car or house, but we won't let go of our
socialist proposal," Sampaio said.[33] Known as a moderate within the
party, Sampaio stressed the PT's history of criticism of Eastern
Europe's communist regimes and insistence on full democracy as
being a necessary condition for socialism: "What is on the agenda of
demands made by the huge rallies in Eastern Europe and what was on
the agenda of the protesters in the Square of Celestial Peace in China is
the democratic question, the participation of civil society in the
elaboration of public policies. That, for us . . . is already a decided

question. Without the permanent participation of organized civil society there is no democracy and, consequently, no socialism."[34]

In addition to presenting a coherent package of economic and social reforms, the PT patched together an alliance with other left parties. Brizola and the PDT quickly decided to back Lula. The small Brazilian Communist Party and its defeated presidential candidate Roberto Freire, as well as many prominent progressive politicians from centrist parties, immediately jumped on the PT bandwagon as well.(Lula's campaign was supported from the beginning by two small parties, the Communist Party of Brazil and the Brazilian Socialist Party, with the alliance dubbed the Brazilian Popular Front. But the two parties played a minor role in the campaign.)

A far greater problem was gaining the support of the PSDB and their candidate for president, Mario Covas who finished fourth in the first round with about 10 per cent of the vote. The party, moderately left of center, was afraid of the PT's call for large-scale agrarian reform and also opposed Lula's insistence on an immediate debt moratorium. But of primary concern were PT documents which pointed to a key role for unions and extra-official organizations in decision-making, an important aspect of the party's ideal of "democratic socialism."

A document prepared for the PSDB by a group under the leadership of economist Edmar Bacha, a formulator of the Cruzado Plan, said "The most general, and important, problem [with the PT's program] is with the conception of 'popular democracy.' It is a conception of the organization of society in which organized workers are placed above the state apparatus and constituted powers, conditioning and leading their actions." The PT was anxious for the support of the party, knowing it would make it difficult for Collor to portray Lula's supporters as dangerous, sectarian radicals. After weeks of negotiations, and some minor compromises by the PT, the PSDB finally announced its official backing for Lula. With the Social Democratic Party's support, Lula's campaign had the backing of the entire spectrum of left-of-center forces – the first time in the country's history that the entire left was united behind a single candidacy. In addition to its alliance-building, the PT also launched a full-scale attack on Collor, and pointed out the questionable sincerity of his professed concern for the poor. After Lula won a place in the runoff, party president Luís Gushiken said, "We're going to reveal Collor for what he is: a representative of the right-wing elite, closely linked to bankers, large landholders and big businessmen." The PT was helped in this endeavor by worried businessmen who, to the horror of Collor, publicly announced their backing for his campaign. The PT hit Collor hard on this support and exposed his ties to Roberto Marinho, Antonio Carlos Margalhães, then minister of Communications and past lackey of the generals, Amazonino Mendes, governor of Amazonas state who once offered to hand out chainsaws to clear the rainforest, and other powerbrokers.

Church support was again crucial to Lula's runoff effort. The CNBB officially declared itself neutral. But it released a profile of the "ideal candidate" as one who "guarantees land reform, workers' rights and social justice," all prominent banners of the PT's campaign.

Others were more overt in their support. Risking the wrath of the Pope, many priests and bishops openly campaigned for Lula. Bishop Mauro Morelli of Duque de Caxias, a poor city on Rio's outskirts, appeared at campaign rallies and on television spots. "Brazil is in a state of war, and in war you have to take sides. I want to take the side of the poor, whom Lula represents," he said. Morelli labelled Collor a candidate "produced by the system to maintain the status quo."

Other prominent activists who backed Lula were Bishop Casaldáliga, Frei Betto (a Dominican friar who was jailed for four years by the generals for organizing opposition to the regime), and leading liberation theologist, Leonardo Boff, who was sentenced by the Pope to a year's "obedient silence" in 1985 for his criticism of the Vatican. Boff said the second-round vote was "between labor, represented by the candidate of the PT, and capital, personified by Collor."

Work at the grassroots level took place nationwide. A lay Catholic group in rural São Paulo state produced a pamphlet, similar to many others distributed throughout the interior, explaining why they supported the PT. Some reasons listed were: "Lula is concerned with the country's distribution of riches and not accumulation for the few. Lula's past is clean and he always struggled on behalf of the working class. Lula represents the new and change. He never was tied to the current government." On the other hand, the pamphlet said, "Collor is a capitalist. And capitalism is responsible for the misery of the people. Collor is rich and a boss. And he always defended the interests of the bosses versus the workers. Collor is allied to international bankers and will continue sending our riches to foreigners. Brazil deserves more than a farcical and dishonest president."

Pastoral Land Commission activists played a key role in the campaign as well. The Commission's chairman in Tocantins state, Adilar

Daltoe, said in an interview at the time, "Lula is a great step forward because he backs agrarian reform, which Collor only pays lip-service to. The choice is clear." (Daltoe denied that Church activists were replacing the *coronels* as the region's vote-getters, as many conservatives claimed. He pointed out that priests and Church lay workers are directly involved in community organizations fighting for basic social services and social reform. "The Church would only be abusing its power if it had its own political party. And we don't buy anybody's vote," he said. He also stressed that he was speaking as an individual, not as a member of the CPT, which did not take an official position but was clearly sympathetic to Lula.)

Collor sought to counter Lula's support from the progressives by appearing on TV and at northeast campaign stops with Damião de Bozzano, a 91-year-old, almost-blind (and apparently senile) mystical priest with tremendous popularity in rural areas. And leaders from the conservative wing of the Church, while generally avoiding endorsements of Collor, were sharply critical of Lula. Bishop Bonaventura Kloppenburg of the southern city of Novo Hamburgo said, "I'm against Lula because I don't want a dictator. Socialism only works in a republic of angels, but we live in a republic of men." Other conservatives criticized progressive activists, saying the Church had no business involving itself directly in party politics, a position which has been repeatedly voiced by Pope John Paul II. Assistant Bishop José Carlos de Lima Vaz of Rio said, "The Church shouldn't be a political actor. The conservatives are the real progressives because they want the Church's mission to remain pure – converting people, bringing them hope, and respecting their liberty." But, as Morelli pointed out, at least some of the traditionalists were guilty of hypocrisy: "Several of the Pope's aides are supporters of Italy's Christian Democratic Party, and the Pope himself has tremendous influence in Eastern Europe. Furthermore, the Church has always been involved in politics. Unfortunately, it has usually been on the wrong side," he said.

(The conservatives, though still a minority in the Church, have seen their strength grow in recent years as the Vatican has been threatening and punishing the progressives and selecting many new bishops from amongst the ranks of the traditionalists. If the Pope succeeds in breaking the control of the progressive wing, a good deal of popular organizing in Brazil, especially in the interior, will be put in jeopardy. The Vatican's efforts to break the power of the Brazilian Church will be discussed in more detail in Chapter 8.)

Key support also came from well-known intellectuals and just about every well-known musician in the country. Stars such as Caetano Veloso, Chico Buarque, Gilberto Gil, Djivan, and scores of others performed free at Lula's campaign stops and on his TV programs.

Lula picked up momentum as election day neared, with huge crowds drawn to his rallies and polls showing him cutting sharply into Collor's lead. Lula's aide Ricardo Kotscho said the people who attended the PT's rallies were "not there only to hear but to actively participate in the largest political manifestations ever registered in the history of the country." And, as Lula told the crowds, "They aren't afraid of me, who alone is no one. They're afraid of you."

On December 13, four days before the vote, some 400,000 people packed the center of Rio for Lula's final public rally. A poll released that night showed him trailing Collor by only one point, 46 to 45 per cent, a technical tie as the survey had an error margin of 3 per cent.

As Lula picked up steam, hysteria among the elite – rampant speculation, with the value of gold and stocks climbing steeply – reached critical mass, as the rich saw their hegemony threatened for the first time ever." On December 11, the dollar on the illegal but widely tolerated black market soared in value against the new cruzado by 25.7 per cent, an all-time record for a single day's gain. (The dollar's climb on the black market, which had also occurred when Lula's poll position strengthened in the first round, was dubbed the "star effect" – because of the PT's symbol – by the press.) And *O Globo*, in a front-page editorial a week before the vote – which appeared next to a story on a poll which showed Lula closing on Collor – warned the country was "on the path to fascism."

But Collor, with a little help from some very powerful friends, had already taken steps to reverse his plunge in the polls. On December 11, he appeared on a television news program, seen in many major cities, that was hosted by a rabid right-winger, Fereira Neto. Lula was also invited, as required by law – Neto sent his campaign headquarters a telex five hours before the program began, when he was 1,000 miles from the TV studio where the show was taped. Needless to say, Lula was unable to attend.

During the program, Collor dropped his social-democrat pose and adapted a fierce anti-communist rhetoric, designed to scare middle-class voters away from Lula. "The Workers Party is going to stain our green-and-yellow flag with red and curse when the national anthem is played," Collor said. He also warned that Brazilians who lived in large apartments would have to cede a bedroom to PT activists if Lula won office. (Collor's claims, given great play by Globo, that Lula and the PT were enemies of democracy were absurdly hypocritical: Collor never raised a peep of protest against Brazil's military dictatorship while Lula had spent time in jail for his activities to bring about the return of civilian rule.)

The following night Miriam Cordeiro, an ex-girlfriend of Lula's and mother of his illegitimate – and acknowledged – fifteen-year-old daughter Lurian, went on nationwide TV and accused him of offering her money to get an abortion. "When she was born, I put her in my lap and said, 'Now go ahead and kill her, because when she was in my belly I wouldn't let you,'" she said.

A high campaign official in Collor's camp resigned the following day, charging Cordeiro with having been given the equivalent of $23,000 for her testimony and calling her former boss's aides "corrupt and dirty." Though Collor officials denied they had paid for the hatchet job, Cordeiro had made none of the charges in an April interview with *Jornal do Brasil*, when she said Lula was thrilled when Lurian was born. Another sign that Cordeiro's testimony was not purely spontaneous is that as late as May 1990 she was still at a luxury hotel in São Paulo, courtesy of the PRN, and had her expenses taken care of by Collor's party. (PRN officials claimed this was necessary as Cordeiro needed to be protected from assassination attempts by crazed PT activists.)

Cordeiro's testimony shocked the country. *Folha de São Paulo* columnist Janio de Freitas wrote that Collor's use of Cordeiro showed "a lack of political and personal decorum without equal in Brazilian electoral history – perhaps in Brazilian political history in general."[35] *Jornal do Brasil* writer Ricardo Noblat (fired after the election, some say for his columns criticizing Collor) captured Collor's essence well: "What he has done in the last few days . . . shows the measure of his personality. Collor is a politician capable of anything – but anything – to reach his objectives. He may even get elected. But what sort of president will he be?"[36] (*O Globo*, naturally, defended their candidate. In a front-page editorial, the paper said, "The practice of democracy recommends that the public knows everything possible about its public men, to better judge them at election time." The paper failed to explain why the public did not have a right to know about Collor's shady political history, which it had tried to suppress. In marked contrast to their treatment of Collor, Marinho's properties often reported on "scandals" the PT was said to be involved in, no matter how flimsy the evidence.)

The direct impact of Cordeiro's charges was probably not great. Brazil is not the United States when it comes to the public's concerns about a candidate's sex life – Gary Hart, the US senator whose 1988 presidential bid was destroyed when he was caught frolicking with model Donna Rice, would have no problems running for president here. Also, many Brazilian women, especially poor ones, have had a child out of wedlock and millions of others have had abortions, though they are technically illegal except in the case of rape or health risk.

The indirect effect, however, was great. Lula was deeply shaken, particularly after Lurian sank into a serious depression. His apathy showed on December 14, when the two candidates ended the period of official campaigning with a three-hour debate televised on all major networks. Collor made absurd charges, claiming, for example that Lula had a sophisticated stereo system that he himself was unable to afford. This was despite the fact that Collor has a huge mansion in Brasília and is a multimillionaire. But, just as at many other moments during the evening, Lula didn't challenge Collor on the issue and point out his obvious lack of sincerity. After all, if he didn't have a stereo, Collor could certainly buy one, and is far wealthier than Lula, who lives in a working-class neighborhood outside São Paulo. Despite Lula's below par performance – he had, according to polls, easily defeated Collor in an earlier debate – most analysts declared the outcome a draw, as Collor also failed to impress.

But the following night, in the most blatantly dishonest act of the entire campaign, and one that had a significant impact on the outcome, TV Globo ran a selection of highlights of the debate that was grossly unfair to Lula. Collor was shown at his best, giving lengthy replies to questions from journalists. Meanwhile, the network picked Lula's worst moments, when he stumbled over words or rubbed his hands together nervously. A network editor who worked on the debate sequence told *Jornal do Brasil*, "I never did dirtier work in my life." After the highlights, Globo ran a poll which showed Collor had won the debate by a crushing margin. Anchorman Cid Moreira neglected to mention that the survey had been conducted by Vox Populi, Collor's own polling firm. Nor did he reveal that 48 per cent of respondents were Collor supporters while only 27 per cent backed Lula.

Directors of several of the country's major polling institutes agreed Globo's presentation of the debate had a far greater impact on the electorate than the event itself. The Gallup institute conducted a survey the day after the debate, in which respondents gave Collor victory by a slim three-point margin. On Saturday, the day after Globo's report, Collor was selected the winner by a margin of 48 to 32 per cent. General election polls showed the same trend. Two Friday surveys showed the candidates running neck and neck. A Saturday poll had voters flocking into Collor's camp after a steady drop for the previous ten days. (The PT asked for free television and radio time to respond to Globo's coverage of the debate, but the Superior Electoral Court turned the request down.)

Another factor that may have helped Collor was the kidnapping of a major Brazilian businessman, Abilio Diniz, by a group of suspected Latin American leftists, mostly Chileans, who reportedly had ties with that country's Movement of the Revolutionary Left. Diniz was kidnapped on December 11, but the case was not publicized until Friday, two days before the election. On that day, police arrested several suspects in the case, and surrounded a house in São Paulo where the rest of the kidnappers were holding Diniz. Police presented to the press materials they found in an apartment rented by the kidnappers. Prominently featured was PT campaign material, on a table alongside weapons, ammunition, and other equipment used by the kidnappers. Police at the scene told reporters that an agenda with names of PT militants was also found. All day Saturday, live flashes were shown on TV of police surrounding the house where Diniz was being held, and São Paulo Archbishop Arns negotiating with the kidnappers.

TV Globo, still under heavy attack over its coverage of the debate, exercised restraint. But many radio and some TV commentators speculated as to whether the PT might be involved in the case, though no proof of such a connection existed. Diniz was released unharmed at 5 p.m. on election day, just as polls closed. Though there was still no proof of any PT connection with the case (nor was any ever uncovered), some newspapers in small rural towns had screaming headlines on Sunday morning saying the PT had kidnapped Diniz. (Months after the release of Diniz – and, of course, months after the election – Maria Regina Braga, the owner of the apartment building where police had seized the PT campaign materials, told a judge that police had also taken from the apartment a good quantity of Collor de Mello's campaign literature, which had never been presented to the press or anyone else.) Lula later said he suspected the Diniz kidnapping may have been a campaign "dirty trick." "It was a game with marked cards, because the police knew [about the kidnapping] since Monday, but waited [for five days] to go public. I think one day the truth about the kidnapping will be told." That may sound like a paranoid version of "sour grapes," but based on past experience, such as the Leme incident in 1986, and the more recent "Lubeca Case," he had reason to be suspicious.[37]

The PT certainly made mistakes in the campaign's final days. Lula's schedule leading up to the final debate was crazily overbooked, so that he had almost no sleep in the days before an event that had been billed as decisive. Many also felt that Lula should have reacted more sharply to Collor's use of Miriam Cordeiro. The only real response was a brief appearance on the PT's campaign spot the following day, where he appeared with his daughter, a PT militant, and said Lurian's opinion of him was the only one that mattered. (Of course, long-term strategic mistakes were made as well. In early 1990, Federal Deputy José Genoíno said the PT had failed to respond effectively to the events sweeping Eastern Europe as the campaign took place – popular revolts were underway throughout the former Soviet bloc, and the Berlin Wall fell in early November. Footage from the event was shown on a number of right-wing candidates' television spots, accompanied by attacks on the PT. The campaign did not respond well, and failed to point out the parallels between its own past struggles and those being waged by the opposition movements in Eastern Europe. "Who should have capitalized on the movements in Eastern Europe was . . . the PT, which was born combating orthodoxy," Genoíno said. He pointed out that Lula was the first Brazilian leftist leader to meet with Lech Wałęsa, when the latter was head of Solidarity in the early 1980s.[38])

On election day, the right took no chances. Private bus companies kept their vehicles off the street in areas of three major cities, Rio de Janeiro, Salvador and Fortaleza, all PT strongholds. Some of these buses were reportedly sent to the interior to take Collor's backers to vote. Other schemes to transport voters, strictly prohibited by election law, were mounted in a number of rural regions. In Alagoas, the powerful sugar barons sent out trucks to haul Collor's backers to the polls. In Roteiro, eighty-five kilometers from Maceió, the poorest county in the state, trucks belonging to the Destilaria Roteiro plantation provided transportation to hundreds of voters. (The town has one telephone, no sewage system, and half the population of 7,000 is illiterate. Most of the town's residents work for the sugar company, as cane-cutters.) The driver of one truck, Cicero Figueiredo, told one newspaper, "As well as this vehicle, there are seven more and a bus. Everybody here is a Collor voter."[39]

With tactics such as these, Collor and the right managed to secure their triumph, with the conservatives garnering 35 million votes against 31 million for Lula. While the PT was trounced in the rural north, the votes in the region only account for 13 per cent of the national total. The election was lost in São Paulo, where the labor movement, but also capital, is strongest. Final votes from the state had Collor ahead by 50.1 to 36.4 per cent, a difference of about 2.5 million votes (60 per cent of the four million vote difference between the candidates. The total does not add up to 100; the rest of the votes were blank, void, or no shows.) Part of the reason was the PT's occupation of City Hall. "The São Paulo militants didn't have the same drive as in other places. . . . Here our people had to justify the bus, the holes in the street, the trash," Lula later said.[40]

Lula ran far ahead in a majority of important state capitals. and won the statewide vote in Rio de Janeiro (64 to 24 per cent), Rio Grande do Sul (59 to 27 per cent), the Federal District, which includes Brasília (53 to 31 per cent), and Pernambuco on the northeastern Atlantic coast (40 to 39 per cent). In addition to running strong in the southern state of Santa Catarina (just losing by 42.7 to 42.2 per cent), Lula picked up substantial support in a number of other northeastern states including Bahía (33.6 versus 35.9 per cent for Collor), Ceará (33.4 to 44.1 per cent), Rio Grande do Norte (37.1 to 41.2 per cent), and Paraíba (34.5 to 42.1 per cent). Overall, Lula received close to half the valid votes in the region.

Reflecting Collor's weak showing in major cities, there were no large victory celebrations. This was especially striking as the vote formally ended the transition to civilian rule, and was also in marked contrast to the case in neighboring Chile where Patricio Alywin won office in a vote held three days prior to Brazil's. One million residents packed the streets of Santiago to celebrate. Long-time residents of Rio, where Lula won by a 3–1 margin, said the post-election mood was even worse than the depression that grips the city if the Brazilian soccer team is eliminated from World Cup tournaments – considered a national tragedy.

But in addition to Lula's 31 million votes, there was other encouraging news. The PT's success at reaching the rural poor during the campaign was a watershed. For the first time ever, a large segment – though, crucially, not a majority – of the northeastern peasantry ignored the wishes of the landowners and actively backed the PT's campaign. Unfortunately, standard scare tactics by Collor's campaigners in the region still proved effective with many peasants. One northeastern migrant who moved to São Paulo but lost his job after Collor announced an austerity program upon taking office, told the *Jornal do Brasil* he had no regrets about voting for the new president. "It would have been worse if the communist had won," he said. "They told us that the foreigners would come and take our lands, and that there would be civil war."[41]

Any claim that the election result was an ideological victory is extremely suspect, for reasons discussed above. First, Collor advocated free-market economic reforms but they were not the centerpiece of his campaign. Far more prominent were his promised war on corruption, attacks on Sarney, and pledges to work for social justice.

Second, Collor's two strongest bases of support were the rich, who certainly did cast anti-socialist votes, and the far more numerous rural poor. Lula admitted after the vote, "The naked and raw truth is that who defeated us, on top of the media, were the less informed and most disfavored sectors of society." Most of that section of the population did not cast ideological votes, but bought Collor's promised "moralization of government" pitch and his promises of income redistribution. Federal Deputy Paulo Delgado incisively noted that Collor's electors were "those who know him [the rich] and those who don't [the poor]. The first supported him because they think he'll change nothing; the second because they think he'll change everything."

Finally, the country's elite exercise a tremendous ability to manipulate the electoral process and, crucially, dominate the media to an even greater degree than their counterparts in most other capitalist countries. What the Brazilian vote really proved is that democratic election laws in an extremely inegalitarian society do not ensure democracy. That doesn't mean Lula would have won in a truly "democratic" vote (if such a thing exists). There were a number of relatively honest, dignified candidates, of various ideological stripes, that ran for the Brazilian presidency. Collor, however, was not among them, and could never have been elected if not for the advantages that accrued to him by virtue of being the establishment's candidate.

NOTES

1. *Folha de São Paulo*, January 8, 1990.

2. Radical liberation theologist Leonardo Boff, who ultimately was a strong backer of Lula, initially flirted with the idea of supporting Covas. In a 1988 interview with one of the authors, he worried that Brazil was not ready for Lula, and did not trust the populism of Brizola. He said Covas's style of politics was "modern" and that he was one of the few candidates who would represent a clean break with the past.

3. Even after Covas made a highly publicized speech during the presidential campaign, saying Brazil needed a "shock of capitalism," he was unable to attract substantial business support. Their failure to rally to Covas is extremely revealing as to the Brazilian establishment's absolute lack of vision. He was clearly not intending to rock the boat too severely; he was honest, and could have been expected to institute mildly progressive reforms without extracting too high a price from businessmen. But the right, and much of the center, preferred to support Collor, who was seen as being more reliable. They chose to ignore his unpredictability, his demogoguery, and his incompetence as a mayor and a governor. It was a decision many may ultimately regret.

4. Rene Dreifuss, *O Jogo da Direita*, p. 264

5. According to 1988 statistics compiled by the country's Superior Electoral Court, 10 per cent of the population is totally illiterate and another 30 per cent is considered semi-literate. The Court probably used a broad definition of literacy. By the Court's own estimate, only 18 per cent of the population has completed high school. The number of illiterates is especially high in the northeast, with 28 per cent of the population in Collor's home state of Alagoas being considered totally illiterate – the worst figure nationwide.

Another interesting figure provided by the Court: the 1989 vote was the first time 75 per cent of voters would cast a ballot for the presidency.

6. *The New York Times*, January 12, 1987.

7. Profile information from *Jornal do Brasil*, August 20, 1989.

8. Ultraleftists in the union movement created substantial problems for the PT, even though Lula had long criticized their beliefs and tactics. In perhaps the worst example, Cyro Garcia, president of the Bankworkers Union in Rio (tied to a Trotskyite sect), decided to support a strike of civil police officers in Rio by lending them a sound truck. Several of the strike leaders had ties to death squads, and one had once run for public office with the slogan, "The only good bandit is a dead bandit." The move was attacked by many members of the CUT, including Eloi Beneduzzi, president of the Rio confederation, who said the support was given "by people who believe that the revolution is at the doorstep, and every strike is a sign that it has finally arrived."

9. *Veja*, May 10, 1989.

10. *Isto É/Senhor*, May 3, 1989.

11. Ibid.

12. Ibid. Luiz Carlos Vaz, an astute reader of *Folha de São Paulo*, wrote a letter to the newspaper in early 1990 pointing out the hypocrisy of those who accused Brazilian workers, among the lowest paid in the world, of undermining the economy with

excessive wage demands. He pointed out that the newspaper had published statistics showing that while inflation in 1989 was 1,764 per cent, prices in highly oligopolized sectors had increased far more – cement by 2,503 per cent, glass by 3,268 per cent, and paint by 2,730. "Part of the press [accuse] the PT and CUT of provoking agitation in the country. It's an image that may not correspond to reality, but it does form public opinion. . . . The news [of excessive price rises] helps show who are the true rabble-rousers," Vaz wrote.

13. *O Estado de São Paulo*, July 7, 1989.

14. Her popularity began recovering in early 1990. A poll released by the Gallup organization in May showed 26.4 per cent of the city residents considered her administration "good" or "excellent," while 70.4 per cent judged it as "average," "bad," or "terrible." The results in the final three categories were all lumped together under the heading of "disapproval." "Average" does not seem to merit condemnation, though, and based on other polls by different organizations, that is the category where a large share of the 70.4 per cent classified as negative would be encountered. In any case, her approval rating was far higher than it had been in November 1989, in the last Gallup survey conducted before the presidential election. At that point, it was only 16.8 per cent.

15. *Isto É/Senhor*, October 4, 1989.

16. Lula complained in a November 29, 1989 interview with *Veja* that the PT had long protested against official corruption but never received credit: "When we accused the government of corruption, the connotation given was of radicalism. When it was Collor that spoke, the connotation was of courage, modernity," he said.

17. October 4, 1989.

18. *Sem Medo de Ser Feliz*, p. 20.

19. In the first-round vote, Lula swept the neighborhood with 1,035 votes, over 700 more than Collor. An Electoral Court judge subsequently ruled that the billboard be taken down. Veloso was transferred out of the region by Archbishop José Cardoso Sobrinho, a leading conservative who had clashed bitterly with the liberation theologists in his diocese.

20. Caiados's disastrous campaign – he received less than 1 per cent of the vote in the first round – foreshadowed tough days ahead for the UDR. A new president of the group, Nagib Abudi Filho, was elected in 1990, but he headed a rapidly declining group of affiliates. In São Paulo, 7 of 21 regional offices were closing, and 22 of 55 offices in Minas Gerais had already shut down. *Folha de São Paulo*, May 21, 1990.

21. *Folha de São Paulo*, December 5, 1989. Unfortunately, her prediction turned out to be highly optimistic. Lula lost Acre state in the second round, as well as Xapuri, where Collor's supporters made a major effort, using traditional populist campaign methods.

22. *Jornal do Brasil*, December 16, 1989. Lula also had the luck to win a lottery conducted by the Superior Electoral Court, and had his name placed first on the ballot. Though there is no way of telling how many votes he got as a result, due to voters' confusion because of the number of names on the ballot – combined with the high number of voters who can't read – it certainly helped out. Usually. In one rural community in the state of Pará, Eudes Mattar, a minor candidate who came in last with 162,343 votes – 0.08 per cent of the total – ran a strong second to Collor. He was listed last on the ballot, and PT militants were certain that many illiterates had voted with the ballot paper upside down.

23. *Veja*, November 29, 1989.

24. *Folha de São Paulo*, July 26, 1989.

25. *Jornal do Brasil*, November 20, 1989.

26. *Jornal do Brasil*, January 21, 1990.

27. *Jornal do Brasil*, November 26, 1989.

28. *Folha de São Paulo* journalist Clovis Rossi showed in a February 1, 1990 article the fallacy of the conservative accounting of inflation in Brazil's specific case. As he noted, the public sector deficit was 5.4 per cent of GNP in 1987, and inflation was 366 per cent. In 1988, the deficit fell to 4.2 per cent of GNP, while inflation leapt to 934 per cent. If there was a direct and simple relationship between the two, of course, inflation should have fallen in 1988. Rossi concluded: "I'm not saying that the public sector deficit doesn't cause inflation. . . . What the public accounts say is that other factors should be considered when designing economic packages aimed to combat inflation." Collor would later ignore that advice.

29. Wages in Brazil are still among the lowest in the world. Statistics released at the First International Meeting of Automobile Workers in 1987 in São Paulo, showed a toolmaker earned $15.76 per hour in the US, $10.4 per hour in Germany, $8.6 per hour in Japan, and $1.95 an hour in Brazil. Respective figures for a general helper were $13.20, $7.15, $6.00, and $0.73. Based on these figures, it was computed that it would take the average-paid worker in the US three months to earn enough money to buy the cheapest car made by American companies, while his Brazilian counterpart would have to work 20.5 months to buy the cheapest Brazilian-made car. *Jornal do Brasil*, May 7, 1990.

30. Collor made the same promises, but backtracked after winning office. He did cut down the number of military cabinet positions, but the armed forces still have three, one each for the army, navy, and airforce, and he only reorganized the intelligence service, placing a civilian in charge and giving the agency a new name, the Secretariat of Strategic Affairs. Meanwhile, the military continues to carry out its own "intelligence" work, and news reports said the SNI's files were turned over to the army.

31. *Jornal do Brasil*, November 26, 1989.

32. One example: in an interview with the news magazine *Veja*, he said, "Foreign capital has to come to Brazil. . . . The only restriction that we make is that there has to be greater control over foreign capital. We can't permit certain forms of profit remissions. The truth is that foreign companies came here and gave better conditions to workers than national companies." (November 29, 1989)

33. *Jornal do Brasil*, November 26, 1989.

34. Ibid.

35. *Folha de São Paulo*, December 15, 1990.

36. *Jornal do Brasil*, December 15, 1990.

37. *Sem Medo de Ser Feliz*, p. 109.

38. *Jornal do Brasil*, March 11, 1990.

39. *Folha de São Paulo*, December 18, 1989.

40. *Sem Medo de Ser Feliz*, p. 97.

41. *Jornal do Brasil*, April 22, 1990.

8

The Road Ahead

It's important not to forget what we won in the campaign. Tell me: ten years ago, what was the PT? What was the popular movement, the union movement? What were the so-called progressive sectors of society?

Lula, February 23, 1990[1]

In Brazil, there's a need to be Jacobin. . . . The PT is going to be a radical party, in the sense that a radical party is needed to make transformations. It's a socialist party. Not social-democratic, not capitalist.

Secretary-General José Dirceu[2]

The prospects for Brazil, and the PT, largely depend on what Collor does in office. Despite his past, Brazil's new president is personally and politically unpredictable, as was seen in his early days in office. On March 16, the day after being sworn in as president, he launched an economic "shock" plan that turned the country on its head. The plan, which was passed largely intact by Congress, contained a mixture of orthodox and heterodox measures, leaning towards the former. The overall intent seemed to be to streamline and rationalize Brazilian "jungle capitalism," and insert the country more squarely into the international economy (with a first step of throwing the economy into a sharp recession).[3]

The heart of the package was a freeze on all bank savings deposits of more than the equivalent of $1,200 and a limitation on withdrawals from the "overnight" market of $600, or 20 per cent of an account, whichever was greater. The freeze hit individuals and corporations, including Brazilian subsidiaries of multinational firms. (The "overnight" is similar to US money-market deposits, and is used by the government to fund its budget deficit. But while US money markets pay about 8 per cent annually, "overnight" deposits were paying up to 100 per cent monthly in the months before Collor took office, a rate necessary to compensate for rampant inflation).[4]

The plan also promised conservative measure such as the privatization of state-run firms, firings of public employees, and the slashing of import tariffs and barriers. But Collor also instituted some measures that have long been favoured by the left, including the PT. These included steep new taxes on wealthy individuals and businesses (including taxes on agricultural production, and financial transactions), as well as an end to bearer accounts, which had allowed for tremendous financial speculation. (These were similar to Swiss bank accounts, where the owner is not required to identify himself. Banks, in fact, had advertised these accounts on TV, saying owning one was "just like being in Switzerland!") Collor also cut billions of dollars in subsidies and fiscal incentives to the private sector.

The bank freeze took an estimated $115 billion out of circulation overnight – about 80 per cent of all bank deposits – and immediately had the economy on the brink of a major recession. Private economists estimate industrial production plunged 20 per cent during the plan's first month, and hundreds of thousands of workers lost their jobs.

Those hit hardest initially – other than the unemployed – were the rich and middle class, who had their assets confiscated by the government. Brasília housewife Maria Laila sent a note to Economy Minister Zelia Cardosa de Mello saying, "For the love of God, liberate my miserable money." Antonio Ermirio de Morães, director of Votorantim Industries, one of the country's leading business groups, had $500 million of his own and his company's money caught in the bank freeze. He later managed to get $200 million out, by paying off back taxes and debts with frozen funds, as government rules allowed. Other companies resorted to illegal methods. For example, blocked funds could be donated to charities, and some firms made deals where they made large contributions but received part of the money back. By the end of the plan's second month *O Globo* reported that "companies [had] unblocked practically all of the money frozen by the Collor Plan."

Brazil's rich felt betrayed by Collor, especially as they had backed him so enthusiastically just months earlier to head off the specter of a leftist government. According to the newsweekly *Veja*, at least two deaths resulted directly from the "New Brazil Plan." A São Paulo lawyer identified only as "Walter Z.," who had his entire life's savings guarded in a bank and was unable to pay debts after most of it was frozen, shot himself three weeks after the plan was decreed. And 39-year-old Altair Rodrigues, a married father of two who had almost all proceeds frozen from the sale of his São Paulo home and bar, died of a heart attack.[5]

A joke then making the rounds revealed the degree of anger many rich Brazilians felt towards Collor. As the story went, a businessman was waiting in a huge bank line in Brasília, the capital, filled with irate customers trying to sort out their financial affairs. The bank manager was observing the queue when the businessman blew up, screaming, "That's it! I'm going to kill Collor." An hour later he was back at the bank, explaining to the manager, "The line was longer at the presidential palace."

But when the smoke had cleared, it became clear that a good share of the price for the "shock" plan was going to be paid by the poor and working class. One of the industries hardest hit by the measures was civil construction. In São Paulo, almost all workers in the sector are northeastern migrants, who had come south to escape that region's poverty. Most work for less than $100 per month and sleep and eat at the job site. But with the industry in near-collapse in the first months after the plan, thousands of migrants were returning home – in the midst of a major drought in the northeast.

Overall unemployment soared, and in São Paulo alone grew by 14 per cent in the plan's first full month, with almost 1 million workers on the street and another 350,000 on collective holiday. The Inter-Union Department of Statistics and Socio-Economic Studies, a labor research group, said the initial impact of the plan had reduced the minimum salary to the equivalent of only $50 per month, its lowest real level since the index was created in 1940. By the end of the year, inflation was already back to a monthly rate of about 20 per cent per month and the country's GNP declined by 4.6 per cent in 1990, the worst fall since records began in 1947. It appears that Brazil is headed towards the same path as that followed by other countries who have carried out free-market "shock" plans, such as Bolivia, Mexico, and Israel: persistent inflation, but at lower levels than those recorded prior to the implementation of austerity measures, accompanied by an extended period of little or no economic growth.

However, Collor does have several factors working in his favor.

First, it wouldn't take much to be a "great" president in Brazil. The economy can hardly get much worse than it was during the Sarney years and very little spending on social programs could earn a tremendous amount of goodwill. Also the elite seem to fear the Collor administration may be their last chance. If reforms aren't accepted now, there is a real chance that a leftist government, whether led by the PT or another party, will take power in 1994, the date of the next presidential balloting.

Second, Collor will certainly have the strong backing of Globo and most of the rest of the media. Shortly after the presidential election, Globo ran a profile of the president-elect that was remarkably fawning, even by its own craven standards. *Folha de São Paulo* columnist Clovis Rossi wrote the day after it ran, "I learned as a child in catechism class that only God is a perfect being . . . [the profile] taught me another perfect being exists, named Fernando Collor de Mello. I got choked up seeing the pile of good qualities Globo was able to attribute to him." Rossi, writing before the fall of Romania's dictator Nicolae Ceausescu, said the program made him "so proud of being Brazilian, and especially a journalist," that he intended to send a tape to Bucharest so the dictator could hire Globo to replace Romanian state TV.[6]

Third, Collor will get as much help as possible from the United States, which was horrified by the prospect of a Lula victory. Under the PT, Brazil could have established a positive alternative economic model for the region and begun to play an important pro-Third World diplomatic role. (Considering the country's size and economic strength, it has very little influence on the international scene.) Collor has made clear he wants close ties with the USA, and Foreign Minister José Francisco Rezek said upon taking office that he wanted to do away with the "Third-Worldism" of Brazilian foreign policy.

But if Collor fails to implement meaningful social reforms and attempts to promote economic growth only by "rationalizing" Brazilian capitalism (Franklin Roosevelt's New Deal without the welfare state), he is likely to permanently lose the support of the poor. Brazil's state sector is extremely corrupt, and in many cases inefficient. Cutting it, and adapting other "free-market" reforms, may ultimately produce short-term economic growth at the expense of even greater economic inequality. In Chile, where the economy finally began growing in the mid 1980s after a decade of Pinochet-promoted Milton Friedman-style programs (and two enormous recessions) poverty is far worse than it was in the early 1970s. And the Chile of 1973, at least compared to the Brazil of 1990, had relatively decent social indicators. Increased poverty in Brazil could blow the lid off an already dangerous situation. All the favorable media coverage in the world won't bail Collor out if that happens. Globo did its best to sell Sarney, but he ended his term as the most unpopular president in Brazilian history.

If Collor indeed tries to run a more progressive administration, the chances are that he will falter when push comes to shove. Even by Latin American standards, the Brazilian upper classes are notorious for their greed and moral corruption. As a local saying goes, the rich "would rather risk all five fingers than give up one ring," and it is unlikely that Collor, for ideological reasons as well as his personal background, will take them on. It's also hard to imagine Collor being too diligent in attacking poverty, as it is precisely the ignorance caused by poverty that allows the elite to remain atop the social pyramid – via such methods as "democratic elections" in which a large chunk of the poor vote for a huckster like Collor.

The PT will be in a good position to pick up the pieces if Collor stumbles. The party emerged from the election greatly strengthened and as the only left-of-center party with a strong base of support in every region of the country. The presidential campaign showed the PT had indeed become a national party, and had penetrated deep into the heart of the interior. Just after the election, press aide Kotscho described one campaign swing, and its significance:

> We couldn't believe the scene from the window of the plane, which in one hour had taken us from [the Amazonian city of] Manaus to the heart of the forest. Even there, in Balbina, an enclave of the construction industry in the middle of the Amazon jungle, where we would film scenes for the People's Network [the party's TV spots] about the environmental damage caused by the construction of a hydroelectric dam, a few dozen men, women and children waved their flags with the star – the star that accompanied us wherever we went, in more than 200 cities in all states. By Jeep or on foot, those militants had got by [the company's] security guards to participate in a ritual that during the entire year repeated itself through-out the whole country: to embrace their candidate and speak of their dreams, their demands, their complaints about life and work in that region. . . . In ten years, the small PT had arrived where political scientists and commentators could never have imagined: in the most distant villages,

where half a dozen Brazilians had organized to fight for their rights and a more dignified life.[7]

And, indeed, the 1989 presidential election also showed that Brazil's poor majority are becoming more politicized and class conscious. In 1982, Lula had run for governor of São Paulo state and used as his campaign slogan, "A Brazilian Like You." After the election, which Lula lost, party leaders decided the slogan had backfired as many poor Brazilians, feeling themselves incapable of exercising leadership, concluded someone with the same class background must be similarly incapable. In 1986, Eduardo Suplicy, a polished, elegant upper-class intellectual, ran as governor of the state (he also lost) and party members joked his slogan should be, "A Brazilian You'd Like to Be." In the 1989 presidential campaign, Lula appealed openly, and effectively, to lower-class voters by recounting his poor upbringing and asked them to "elect a worker for president, for the first time in Brazil's history." Though there are still many poor Brazilians who wouldn't vote for Lula because he wasn't "cultured" or "educated," the tactic was largely successful this time. A major reason for this is that the PT, through its own political activities, has proved the poor can make their own history.

Party leaders have said they have much to discuss in the coming years, especially after the changes that swept Eastern Europe in 1989, but state emphatically that the PT will remain a radical party. Secretary-General José Dirceu said after the election, "The PT doesn't want to be a social-democratic party because we're against capitalism."

However, many party leaders do seem intent on rethinking some basic tenets, and have become even more critical of (former) communist governments. Federal Deputy José Genoíno, who was long regarded as representing the party's left wing, said in an early 1990 interview, "Let's place the two systems side by side. Capitalism has a history of hunger and misery. We have to denounce that. But at the same time, we also have to denounce the crimes of Eastern Europe. The crimes of the Gulag and the lack of liberty. . . . I think that Gorbachev took an important attitude in breaking with the authoritarian and repressive society in the Soviet Union, where there existed no citizenship or [social] movements."(Genoíno, who as a Communist Party militant in 1972 briefly fought with the guerrilla movement based in the southeastern Amazon, also called for free elections in Cuba.) He said leftists, both in Brazil and elsewhere, were guilty of a serious "misreading of Marx. Postulates should not have been transformed into faith, dogma. . . . The great error of the left was to transform Marxism into an absolute truth."[8]

Independent of the theoretical debate underway, the PT's future will also depend on the future of the independent movements that play such an important part in the party. The CUT, the PT's powerful labor ally, certainly appears to be moving towards better days. A poll conducted in late 1989 showed that the CUT dominated unions in the country's industrial sector, and was far more powerful than its arch-rival CGT (which has received money from the AFL-CIO and the Reagan-created National Endowment for Democracy). The survey, conducted among 500 of the country's biggest firms from 157 industries, found the CUT represented 65.3 per cent of workers, while the CGT represented only 16.3 per cent (the rest were in independent unions). "The most troublesome point, in the opinion of businessmen, is that this tendency will probably be maintained," said economist Julio Lobos, who conducted the survey. Lobos also found that the CUT controlled 89 per cent of the unions in the state sector, 51 per cent in national industries (versus 20 per cent for CGT), and 56 per cent of multinationals (versus 18 per cent for the CGT).[9] Though unions are still relatively weak in Brazil, representing only about 30 per cent of workers in 1990, the CUT's numbers have increased rapidly in recent years and that trend is expected to continue.

The Catholic Church is not directly tied to the PT but its future is also of critical importance to the party. Even the future of the hierarchy – which has a fair number of PT sympathizers but can by no means be considered to be linked to the party in any way – will have an important impact. Changes at the top will greatly effect the situation of grassroots activists and the popular organizations they have helped construct, many of which work closely with the PT. The future of the Brazilian Church is complicated as it depends on both internal developments and, even more importantly, external ones – specifically, its ongoing battle with Rome. In addition to a 1988 warning to Bishop Casaldáliga, the Vatican has taken a number of other measures during recent years to rein in the Brazilian Church. The most important of them includes:

– In 1985, liberation theologist Leonardo Boff received orders from the Vatican to keep "penitential silence" for ten months. His major offense was to have directly criticized the Church hierarchy, which he called "elitist" and "feudal" in his book *Church: Charisma and Power*.

– The Vatican sent "warning letters" to at least five prominent religious leaders in 1988: Cardinal Aloísio Lorscheider of the north-eastern city of Fortaleza, José Maria Pires (one of Brazil's only black bishops) of João Pessoa, Bishop Marcelo Carvalheira of Paraíba, and Adriano Hypolito and Waldir Calheiros, both bishops from dioceses near Rio. The strongest warning was reportedly sent to Hypolito, for "running an irresponsible administration" and "opening paths for ideological groups."[10] (Hypolito was a strong opponent of the military regime, and paid a heavy price for his criticism of the generals. In 1976, he was kidnapped and tortured by members of a right-wing paramilitary group because of his anti-government pronouncements.) Pires was also said to be under heavy fire, especially for closing down a traditional seminary in his diocese and turning it into a training center for lay workers. Called the "Seminary of Hoe Theology," students work the land during the morning .and study during the afternoon.

– In 1989, Cardinal Arns's São Paulo archdiocese was divided into five smaller units, in a clear attempt to lessen his influence. Moderate bishops were appointed in the four newly created dioceses, and Arns was left in control of an area largely populated by the middle class – who are not tremendously fond of his progressive approach.

Over the past few years, the Vatican has also appointed a number of arch conservatives to key dioceses, including Cardinal Lucas Moreira Neves as archbishop in Salvador and Cardinal José Freire Falcão as archbishop in Brasília.

Most observers believe Pope John Paul II is trying to "clean up" the Latin American Church before the 1992 celebration in Santo Domingo, the Dominican Republic, of 500 years of Catholic evangelization on the continent. The Brazilian church, which is certainly the region's most influential, and progressive, is naturally the primary target. (Rome's motivations are not purely based on political disagreements with the country's hierarchy. The Brazilian Catholic Church is the world's third largest, after the Italian and American, and the Vatican is known to be wary of any rivals, either theological or otherwise.)

Bishop Tomás Balduino of the city of Goiás in the central state of the same name, said in a 1988 interview that the Vatican was "determined to restore the centralized and authoritarian structure of the Church – a structure which does not tolerate original thought or any divergence from the traditional doctrine of saving souls." Balduino and his progressive allies still hold a majority in the CNBB, but it is a diminishing one, and some observers say the bishops have already begun to soften their stance towards the powers that be. In fact, criticism of Collor's economic plan was surprisingly timid. Casaldáliga tried to pass a motion condemning the recessive nature of his economic strategy at a meeting of the Church hierarchy in April 1990, but the motion was not approved. Many grassroots militants, especially in rural areas where the protection of the local bishop is of crucial importance (particularly in terms of personal safety for land-reform activists), believe many progressive bishops are feeling the heat. If the Vatican does succeed in breaking the progressives' control of the Church, the consequences could be serious, for both the PT and the rural poor.

LONG-TERM AND THEORETICAL CONSIDERATIONS

Brazil inherited from the military dictatorship and its "Economic Miracle" a social crisis without historical precedent. The model of development imposed by the generals made possible accelerated economic growth and increased integration with the international market, based on technological innovation and the implementation of a production structure oriented towards external demands. The brutal sacrifice this model entailed for the poor majority made Brazil one of the weak links in the Latin American capitalist system. If the country was, on the one hand, at the forefront of economic growth, a time-bomb of internal contradiction was created by the resulting concentration of wealth and corresponding social exclusion.

The PT initially was anchored to that sector of the working class which emerged with the rapid industrial growth of the 1970s. Gathered in its wake was a sub-proletarian mass, today the country's majority, which has no place in the formal production system; a mass which survives on intermittent employment in the informal sector, under concealed or open forms of underemployment, in rural areas and on the periphery of the great urban centers. Such a social scenario has proved to be a breeding ground for the most diverse forms of violence. One of the most insidious, and common, is found in the slums that ring the large cities, where drug dealers, police and businessmen exploit the huge number of poor children for the purpose of organized crime. Such a situation has made the so-called Baixada

Fluminense, a poor area on Rio's outskirts, the most violent area in the world, according to United Nations statistics.

From the military regime through the ineptitude and incompetence of the Sarney government, Brazil's economic and social problems have dramatically worsened. The only apparent solution to the overwhelming ills which now exist appears to be a strong central government with the power to break the strength of entrenched corporate interests, and rebuild and legitimize a new societal equilibrium, allowing for a renewed cycle of economic growth (in short, to create new "social structures of accumulation," in the words of economist David Gordon, such as Franklin Roosevelt's New Deal represented to the United States in the 1930s). Collor's presidency represents an attempt, through a Bonapartist regime, to impose such an equilibrium. His economic plan pursues strategic objectives of crucial interest to Brazilian capitalism: the modernization of the state through a neo-liberal plan and the economy's reinsertion into the international market in accordance with the new international division of labor created in the 1980s (given the space available to the countries on the capitalist periphery). The possibility of "success" resides in Collor's ability to break the resistance of unions and social movements, just as Ronald Reagan and Margaret Thatcher found it necessary to reverse gains made by the working class and the poor in the United States and Britain before fully implementing their respective economic "reforms." A strong recession with an increase in unemployment, income concentration and the reversal of workers' social gains are elements indispensable to the "modernizing" objectives of the Collor government. Privatization of state-owned enterprises, a greater opening to international markets, including the lowering of trade barriers to open the country's economy to increased imports, and new infusions of foreign capital are all integral components of the government's plans.

The main obstacle to these objectives are the level of organization, mobilization and political consciousness of Brazilian popular movements. And, as this capacity for resistance cannot be relegated only to the social realm, at the risk of becoming impotent, the PT's future as the political representative of the organized and politicized sectors of the population is absolutely central to Brazil's destiny in the 1990s. The party's capacity to build a strong alternative to state power, as represented by the Collor government, based on mass support for a coherent development program that promotes the redistribution of wealth, as well as its creation, represents the progressive path away from the crisis in which Brazil finds itself at the start of the decade.

After having been nearly elected president, Lula decided against running for certain reelection to Congress, in order to dedicate himself fully to building the PT on a national level, and, in his words, "prepare the party for the assumption of power." His decision initially stunned party militants (and was also attacked by the nation's media, with many writers accusing him of scorning liberal institutions) but was finally understood, at least internally, as an affirmation that Congress and the institutional political system represent only one aspect of politics. Lula chose to return to the factory gate and the streets to better understand the large segment of the population that remains "apolitical," and to help construct the party starting from where the PT was born ten years ago.

During the 1980s, the decade of neo-liberalism, when political spotlights and ideological spaces were occupied by a rejuvenated right wing, Latin America's most important new political party came from the left, with the PT. When Lula's victory in the 1989 election was a real possibility, Army Minister Leônidas Pires warned that Brazil was "swimming against the current of worldwide tendencies." The minister failed to understand, or chose to ignore, that it is capitalism which has placed Brazil, Latin America and the Third World against "worldwide currents." The PT's consolidation as a real alternative to power merely expresses that fact. The neo-liberal model now in vogue weakens parties, demeans politics, further reduces the electoral process to marketing games and media manipulation, and demobilizes the population – thus, the PT travels against the current.

After having created a country whose majority is impoverished and miserable, Brazil's elite is frightened at the prospect of political and social rebellion. The trajectory of the PT is the concrete manifestation of this specter. The party's 1989 presidential campaign slogan, "Sem Medo de Ser Feliz" ("Without Fear of Being Happy") expresses the audacity of a party which seeks to take power at the head of the huge majority and show that, politically and ethically, the people have the right to happiness. The responsibility of presenting the path toward the realization of this hope lies with political leaders and forces.

The 1990s appear certain to be one of the most important decades in Brazilian history. For the first time, workers' emancipation is within reach. This struggle is part of socialism's renewal and the hope for a society based on equality and justice.

NOTES

1. *Sem Medo de Ser Feliz*, p. 111.
2. *Folha de São Paulo*, December 24, 1989.
3. The press later reported that Collor's economic plan may have been influenced by a study prepared by the Superior War School (ESG), which had been the strategic planner behind the 1964 coup. According to *O Estado de São Paulo*, Collor met in June 1989 with General Oswaldo Muniz Oliva, then head of the institution. The general gave him a study entitled "1990–2000: the vital decade – for a modern and democratic Brazil," which had been prepared by a group of the ESG's permanent staff. At least three other meetings between future Collor appointees (including Economy Minister Zelia Cardoso de Mello and Central Bank President Ibrahim Eris), took place, two during the first round of the election and one just before the runoff vote. Among the ideas proposed in the ESG study were, according to a report of May 5, 1990 in *O Estado de São Paulo*, "the creation of an Infrastructure Ministry, the liberation of the exchange rate for the national currency, the transformation of the National Information Service into a new agency called the Secretary for Strategic Affairs, and even the necessity of a freeze on part of the resources invested in publicly held papers." Coincidentally or not, all these proposals were ultimately contained in the March 16 package. In any case, the fact that military planners had similar ideas in mind show the plan was not the tremendous break with the status quo that Collor and his supporters claimed.
4. By centralizing billions of dollars in the Central Bank, and leaving much of the private sector without money, the Plan created tremendous room for corruption and favoritism. For example, while promising to eliminate all subsidies and incentives, Collor soon reinstituted benefits to the sugar-cane industry under a new name – the "equalization of costs tax." The measure freed $18 million in blocked money for sugar-mill operators. Two of the major beneficiaries were two brothers, Carlos and João Lyra. The latter was the father-in-law of Collor's younger brother, Pedro, and a wealthy senator who provided Collor with several Lear Jets and money for his presidential campaign. While the government said the move was necessary to keep sugar and alcohol fuel costs down, there is no way of knowing whether there were also political considerations taken into account.
   Another troublesome feature of the plan was a controversial measure that subjected managers and owners of companies that commit "crimes against the popular economy" to jail time, with no guarantee of bail. The law, which was subsequently withdrawn and rewritten after a storm of protest, resulted in the arrest of forty-four businessmen. One victim, Antonio Gaspar, manager of a São Paulo supermarket was arrested because the store had allegedly raised prices on two items, of about 10,000 sold. Several bank managers in major cities were also arrested, charged with denying clients the right to withdraw up to the legal maximum from their bank accounts.
   Police also raided the Tama publishing house in Rio, seized copies of the book *Tax Havens*, and charged two of the firm's officials with "inciting tax evasion." Brazil's 1988 constitution prohibits all censorship. Four days later, the prominent *Folha de São Paulo* newspaper was invaded by heavily armed police agents who arrested two company officers for allegedly post-dating an invoice to avoid the currency freeze. The newspaper had published most of the reports during the presidential campaign that accused Collor of corruption during his 1987 to mid-1989 term as governor of the northeastern state of Alagoas. The paper's owner believed the police action was no coincidence. "Not even during the dictatorship were we victims of violence like that," *Folha de São Paulo*'s owner Octavio Frias said.
5. *Veja*, April 18, 1990.

6. *Folha de São Paulo*, December 22, 1989.
7. *Jornal do Brasil*, December 24, 1989.
8. *Jornal do Brasil*, March 11, 1990.
9. *Veja*, November 8, 1989.
10. *Folha de São Paulo*, October 18, 1988.

Interview with Lula

After having received 31 million votes for president in the 1989 election, you decided against running for reelection to Congress. What is the political significance of that decision?

There were various reasons for my decision. First, I never wanted to be a deputy. I wanted to be a member of the constituent assembly, I was, and after having elaborated the new constitution wanted to resign immediately. But during a party evaluation, the *companheiros* decided that if I stepped down it would look like a renunciation, which is never looked upon kindly by the Brazilian electorate.

After the presidential elections, I felt that we had participated in such a great campaign, so extraordinary, that only another presidential campaign would motivate me.

There was also the question of organizing the party. Being a deputy, I would be obliged to be in Brasília [the capital] at least three days a week, which would keep me from travelling throughout the country and building the party, which had grown so much electorally. But the fact that we received so much support in the election doesn't mean we will enjoy the same position in the next elections. The fact that we received all those votes doesn't mean we have the structure to maintain that level of support.

It's important to remember that though I received 31 million votes in the second round, the PT's vote in reality was 12 million votes, which I got in the first round. We received almost triple that in the second round, due to the alliances we built.

The PT needs to reorganize, we need to rebuild the party's bases, at the factory level, at the university level, at the neighborhood level. We need to have tighter policies to build up our activists. To reorganize the party means being available to travel throughout the country.

Another issue that made me decide not to run for reelection is the "Parallel Government."[1] I think there's a need for innovation in playing the role of opposition. You can't just act as an opposition party during an election campaign – that work has to continue when the campaign ends. A party like the PT has a very agitated life: it needs to be directly involved with the social movements, the strikes, the union movement. Because of this dynamic, the PT has a hard time keeping track of the government's actions. I intend to dedicate myself to strengthening the parallel government through a systematic monitoring of the Collor administration, not only to attack what's wrong, but above all to concretely demonstrate to society what the PT would have done if we had won the elections.

The third reason I didn't run for deputy was because I think it's important for the PT to have a greater political profile at the international level, especially in Latin America. The economic integration of Latin America has been defended by all of the continent's rulers for a very long time, but it doesn't happen precisely because the bourgeoisie doesn't want it, because each [national] bourgeoisie, in isolation, wants to profit from good relations with the rich countries. So Brazil only thinks about Brazil, Mexico about Mexico, Argentina about Argentina – each ruling administration thinks only about the best means of profiting from good relations with the First World. This has been going on for the past 500 years and thus far none of these countries has managed to realize the benefits. On the contrary, all have made the maximum amount of concessions, while our wealth is squandered.

I want to dedicate myself to working with leftist sectors in Latin America, to elaborate a new conception of economic integration, to show that there is no individual way out of the crisis we're facing at the international level. And that every time a Latin country tries alone to renegotiate better commercial, economic, or even cultural deals with Europe or the United States, what really happens? It's like placing a lightweight up against Mike Tyson – no matter how good he is, the odds are stacked against him and he ends up getting knocked out.

My decision is also a message to the PT. I think this sequence of elections, which are being held practically every year, can transform the PT into purely an electoral party. My action is one of divestment. I wouldn't have a hard time winning office a second time, the salary is good, the immunity even better, the diplomatic passport is fantastic, but if we acquire the habit of being in power we won't want to give it up. I want to prove to myself, to my party, to public opinion, that it's possible to act politically without needing to constantly be in that crazy fight for power.[2]

I don't want power for Lula. I think that the working class, with or without Lula, will one day take power. The important thing is that the working class knows that. And my gesture, over time, will help to build that awareness.

How was it possible for the PT, a radical, anti-capitalist party that espouses socialism, to win so many votes in a country like Brazil?

I think it happened because it wasn't a last-minute candidacy. My political career and the PT's history have been marked by a very strong commitment to democracy, by a solid and coherent line and by rhetoric that might be radical for Europeans or for the Brazilian upper middle class, but is not radical for the 90 per cent of the people who live in poverty. There were moments during the presidential campaign when Fernando Collor was more radical than I. The things that he said about ex-president Sarney, which in the press appeared as a demonstration of courage, would have been used to attack the PT had I said them. If I had called Sarney "shameless," "a thief," these statements would have become headlines denouncing the PT. Since Collor represents the bourgeoisie and all of that was part of a bourgeois strategy to win the elections,[3] his comments were used favorably, to boost his image. When he insulted the military – if it were me, I'm sure there would have been a week of attacks on socialism, communism, and the PT's radicalism.

In fact, there was no radicalism in our proposal. It was well understood by the politicized section of Brazilian society. We had 31 million votes because of the coherence and the political maturity we demonstrated during the elections.

What repercussions do you think the PT's success could have for the left in other countries?

I think the PT could contribute significantly to the left in Latin America. This left lived on the glory of the 1917 revolution, then on the glory of the Chinese revolution, and then on the glory of the Cuban revolution. Suddenly, that world crumbled. But before that happened, the PT had appeared, saying that it had to crumble. We appeared as a new party, born of the most organized sectors of the working class, led mostly by an enormous contingent of rural workers, factory workers and intellectuals – in other words, by people whose lives were traditionally tied to the working class.

I also think it's positive that groups who think so differently coexist in the PT, even those with antagonistic ideologies and notions about forms of organization. The PT offers a positive experience to other political organizations of how it is possible to coexist with diversity. With our experience, we can make an important contribution to other Latin American organizations; I felt that strongly at the meeting of Latin American organizations we held this July in São Paulo, attended by close to fifty groups.[4]

The PT can live with diversity because it's not a traditional party, not a traditional left. That helps in other ways. They can't just write us off as "Marxists," as "Bolsheviks." All they can say is that the workers who lead the PT are unionists who acquired the consciousness that it was necessary to build a political party. The Brazilian bourgeoisie believed that our candidacy would be easily defeated by their candidate [Collor] in the presidential elections, because they didn't think we would be able to form alliances for the second round.[5] We proved the contrary, we had the ability and political initiative to make these alliances.

What has the PT learned from its experience in municipal government, in some of the country's major cities, since 1989?

I feel free to evaluate and criticize, when necessary, the PT's municipal governments for a very simple reason: I want the PT to reach office, to see if it can meet the demands we make of the government. Because a party begins to mature not when it becomes moderate, but when it gains consciousness of its responsibilities; that is, when it begins to measure what it says in a campaign against what it is going to do after that campaign. And the fact that the PT has governed in some cities is giving it this maturity.

I get tired of arguing with our administrators, telling them they should appoint the most sectarian militants to certain posts – state firms, regional governments – so that they [the militants] become aware that we aren't always capable of doing what we demand of others. I think the PT can meet that challenge, but not with the ease and naivety with which we thought it could be done.

Government administration has made the PT more mature and responsible. Luisa Erundina [the party's mayor of São Paulo] upholds the same ideological strength as always, the same political convictions. She's a woman of strong principles, and she has realized that she has to govern São Paulo, a city of millions, and a far bigger world than that of the PT, its internal factions, its supporters, and its union members. São Paulo includes small and large industrialists, politicized and non-politicized people, people for us and people against us. Given that, the great challenge is to govern by prioritizing work that benefits the oppressed sectors.

It's been a very important lesson for us. In 1988, Plínio de Arruda Sampaio was labeled as reformist, rightist. Two years later, almost unanimously, he was accepted as our party's candidate for governor of São Paulo,[6] precisely because our activists now realize that to govern is not to make speeches, to govern is to do, to perform.

In terms of a political system, do you favor parliamentarianism or presidentialism?[7]

I never agreed that parliamentarianism would solve all of Brazil's problems. I do think it's a more democratic form of government. Government power would become more vulnerable to public opinion, to parliament and to public institutions.

But it's important to take into account that another fundamental issue, beyond the type of regime, is the cultural question. In the United States, the president is vulnerable. A strong president like Nixon fell. Congress is capable of toppling the president, no matter how strong he is. Judicial power is respected.

I think parliamentarianism could cause more frustration in Brazilian society. Because the problem is not the regime, it's the mentality of Brazilian politicians. Brazilian politicians are corrupt, they are lackeys, they can be bought. They behave in Congress as if it were the stockmarket and they were traders – they use it to bargain. What we need, therefore, is to change the cultural behavior of our politicians, our institutions.

For example, when we approved the creation of provisional measures in the new Brazilian constitution, in the great debates that took place, our objective was to put an end to the military regime's legislation by decree.[8] Provisional measures were modeled after [a similar type of law] used in the Italian system, which was said to work well and was guaranteed by the Italian constitution, etc. The problem was that we forgot we don't live in Italy, we don't have Italian politicians or the Italian Parliament. President Collor has constantly used the provisional measure, trivializing its use, when it should be employed only in emergency situations. He tries to show that he doesn't need Congress because the use of the provisional measure creates consumed facts.

It would be terrible to polarize the debate between parliamentarianism and presidentialism, as if one was made by God and the other by the Devil. Either one can work if elected officials had political consciousness, if they were honest, if they had proposals and acted in the best interests of the country, and were not thinking only about the next elections.

Is it really possible for the working class to take power and govern a capitalist society?

Not long ago, I never would have believed it was possible for workers to take power through the vote. Today I do. With a little more organization, the working class can take power in Brazil, and carry out a revolutionary program, from the standpoint of priorities, from the standpoint of the popular involvement of society and in regard to relations with adversaries. There will be problems. But that is part of the greatness of politics – to know how to administer problems, to live with your adversaries and to live with adversity. It's possible for the working class to elaborate a popular democratic program and to put it in action, and to prove that such a program can work.

Our problem is that we live in a country so miserable, the needs of the people are so great, that the people want immediate results. There is so much poverty that it becomes difficult to modernise the country. I've seen the difficulty the mayor of São Paulo has had in trying to put an automatic device in buses to eliminate the faretaker's position. As the country is so poor, and as the faretaker is a salaried worker, people are sure to fight for the maintenance of their jobs. But we can't not modernize the country because of that. We can use these workers in other areas and I think that's the correct approach, not to fire workers but to place them elsewhere, so the country can develop and absorb this labor.

In the light of the changes in Eastern Europe in 1989, and the collapse of the communist governments, what does socialism mean today?

I am totally convinced I have no reason to complain and mourn about what has happened in Eastern Europe, because it's going to be good for socialism. Because the hard truth is that there was no socialism there. The fact is that the ex-leader of East Germany, Erich Honecker, a victim of the Nazis, who was sent to their concentration camps, a lifelong communist, made a mess of things. The bureaucracy, the lack of democracy, the lack of liberty, the impossibility for the people to breathe, the lack of union autonomy – all that shows socialism didn't exist. If a regime is popular, extraordinary, it doesn't need such toughness, such a closure of power to the people.

When the PT was born in 1980, we were already saying that socialism was synonomous with democracy. Without democracy there is no socialism. I still dream of socialism, of a society with just income distribution, where the participation of the people is the fairest and most egalitarian possible, where manual labor is valued, where basic needs of housing and schooling are rights, not privileges.

The criticisms the US government has made about Cuba and the Sandinista government of Nicaragua, the demand that elections be held [are very narrow] . . . real democracy should be demanded for all of Latin America. Because, for myself, democracy isn't just holding elections, the election is just a comma. For me, democracy exists to the degree that everyone has the same opportunities. And in Latin America, while all the nice constitutions guarantee that, the truth is that it doesn't exist. The poor child has no chance of getting a good job, of being a bank manager or a doctor. That's my criticism of [formal] democracy, and I think socialism must be seen in that context.

What was the meaning of the 1989 campaign slogan, "Without Fear of Being Happy"?

This slogan, which was born in the midst of the campaign because it was part of a campaign song, should mean many different things in different countries of the world. The North American people, while having access to material goods and a very good standard of life, have little consciousness of misery in the world, and are accomplices in the current state of affairs, because they are taught to look out for themselves and not for others. If the United States didn't spend $300 billion a year on sophisticated weapons, if this money was instead spent to plant rice, beans, to build schools and hospitals, in short to develop the planet Earth, I think everyone could be a lot happier.

A slogan like ours could lead the North American people to increase their political consciousness, to stop the USA from interfering so much in the destiny of other peoples. The role of the United States could be more peaceful, to produce fewer arms and more jobs.

I think the slogan is important because people are afraid to be happy. People are afraid to believe in the new, to try things that are untested. And we'll never move forward without political will, without audacity, without daring. I hope the slogan leads people to fight for their own happiness.

August 1990

NOTES

1. Set up by the PT in early 1990, to "monitor" Collor's administration. Similar in concept to structures established by opposition parties in parliamentary regimes.

2. The possibility of the PT losing its identity as an activist party, and becoming purely an electoral vehicle for its candidates, has frequently been discussed by party leaders. It is a very real problem, as elections for municipal, state and/or federal offices were held in 1985, 1986, 1988, 1989 and 1990. The very fact that the PT must run candidates in these elections inevitably leads to a diminution in energies spent on grassroots activities. Lula himself was criticized during his 1986-90 term as federal deputy by some who felt he was becoming too moderate and conciliatory with ideological foes. Labor Court judge Almir Pazzianotti once reported that a São Paulo cab driver told him, "I voted for Lula. It's too bad he turned into a deputy."

3. At one moment in the campaign, Collor called Sarney a "son of a whore." *Jornal do Brasil*, the Rio daily, reported in mid 1990 that officials from Collor's campaign met with Sarney staffers between the first- and second-round votes and let them know that Collor was going to unleash heavy verbal artillery against Sarney as part of his electoral strategy. The meeting was held, the newspaper said, so there'd be no hard feelings.

While that may be true, it must be said that Collor genuinely seemed to dislike Sarney, and his attacks on him began well before the meetings reported by *Jornal do Brasil*. That antipathy, though, is likely to be more personal than it is political. While Sarney represents the old-style Brazilian conservative class and Collor represents its "modernizing" wing, the ideological gap between the two is not very broad. One example: While Collor ran for president as a fierce opponent of Sarney and everything he stood for, his congressional base of support during his first year in office was made up of precisely the same parties that had backed the latter.

4. The meeting was held to discuss the left's future in the 1990s. Representatives from about fifteen countries attended, mostly from South America but including delegates from Cuba, El Salvador's Farabundo Martí Liberation Front, and the Dominican Republic.

5. That was certainly Collor's belief. After Lula squeaked past Brizola to win a place in the second round, he and his campaign strategists gloated over their good fortune. They believed Brizola would have been able to win allies from across the political spectrum whereas Lula would be marginalized on the left and thus easy to defeat. As seen in Chapter 7, they were only partly correct; with the exception of the PSDB, Lula was "marginalized" on the left. However, that did not make him an easy opponent.

6. Sampaio's campaign never got off the ground. He finished a distant fourth in the October 25, 1990 elections. That probably had little to do with his ideological positions and a lot to do with the PT's disorganization following Lula's 1989 presidential defeat.

7. Currently a hot debate in Brazil. A nationwide plebescite is scheduled for 1993 to decide if the presidential system is maintained or if a parliamentary system is adopted.

8. The military government created the "decree law," which was submitted to Congress and went into effect immediately, and became law in thirty days if not voted on by legislators (or, obviously, if approved). "Provisional measures," introduced with the 1988 civilian constitution, also went into effect immediately but only became law if Congress approved them; if the measure had not been voted on within thirty days (or if it was rejected) it was considered dead. Furthermore, provisional measures were only to be used in cases of extreme urgency.

Sarney abused the provisional measures as did Collor. The latter used them routinely, issuing more than 150 during his first year in office (including his entire March 16 economic package). Another trick of Collor's was to reissue a provisional measure after it had been voted down by Congress, changing the wording just enough to claim that it was not the same as its predecessor.

Index